Also by Hillary Rodham Clinton

It Takes a Village: And Other Lessons Children Teach Us

Dear Socks, Dear Buddy: Kids' Letters to the First Pets

An Invitation to the White House

At Home with History

HILLARY RODHAM CLINTON

Simon & Schuster

NEW YORK   LONDON   TORONTO   SYDNEY   SINGAPORE

SIMON & SCHUSTER
Rockefeller Center
1230 Avenue of the Americas
New York, New York 10020

SIMON & SCHUSTER and colophon are registered
trademarks of Simon & Schuster, Inc.

Designed by Amy Hill

Manufactured in the United States of America

10 9 8 7 6 5 4 3 2 1

Library of Congress Cataloging-in-Publication Data
Clinton, Hillary Rodham.
An invitation to the White House : at home with history / Hillary Rodham Clinton.
p. cm.
Includes index.
1. White House (Washington, D.C.) 2. White House (Washington, D.C.)—Pictorial
works. 3. Clinton, Bill, date. 4. Clinton, Hillary Rodham. 5. Clinton, Bill,
1946—Pictorial works. 6. Clinton, Hillary Rodham—Pictorial works. 7. Washington
(D.C.)—Buildings, structures, etc. 8. Washington (D.C.)—Buildings, structures,
etc.—Pictorial works. I. Title.
F204.W5 C58 2000
975.3—dc21   00-058323
ISBN 0-684-85799-5

To the American people,

whose commitment to democracy has

made this house more than a home;

and to the White House staff,

whose dedication has made a home

of this venerable house.

CONTENTS

FOREWORD BY *J. Carter Brown*

Walk through the doors of the White House and you enter not just the center of power of the United States and the home of the President and his family, but the setting for one of the most splendid and historic collections of American art and furnishings anywhere in the world. Much of the credit goes to our nation's First Ladies, from Abigail Adams to Hillary Clinton.

Each first family has left its mark on the White House. For much of the 19th century, the focus of the White House art collection was historical, with a particular emphasis on presidential portraiture. But by the end of the century, aesthetics began to play a larger role, and in 1925 Grace Coolidge named a committee to approve gifts of art and furnishings for the executive mansion. The subtle evolution that would turn the White House into a museum had begun.

That evolution culminated in 1961, when Jacqueline Kennedy focused new attention on the White House by appearing before millions of Americans conducting a televised tour. She instituted a professional curatorial office, founded the White House Historical Association (for which I have been happy to serve as treasurer since 1969), and formed what would become the Committee for the Preservation of the White House to advise Presidents and First Ladies on the acquisition and display of historic and artistic objects.

I have been involved with this committee since the end of the Kennedy administration, and, as the director of the National Gallery of Art and chair of the U.S. Commission of Fine Arts, I have had the privilege of working with every President and First Lady since. It has been a special pleasure to advise Mrs. Clinton, whose own style and appreciation for the history of the White House, as well as its art and furnishings, have been evident since the day she first arrived. One of her first requests was to see the paintings in storage, retrieving such treasures as the Whistler *Nocturne.* It was she who pursued the acquisition of the paintings *Bear Lake, New Mexico* by Georgia O'Keeffe and *Sand Dunes at Sunset, Atlantic City* by Henry Ossawa Tanner to fill important gaps in the collection—the O'Keeffe is the first painting by a 20th-century female artist to be prominently displayed on the state floor, and the Tanner is the first painting by an African-American to be included in the permanent collection. She also helped procure the gift of the wonderful Gilbert Stuart portrait of Dolley Madison.

Above: The U.S. Army Herald Trumpets on the South Portico on Flag Day, June 14, 1993.

Mrs. Clinton, a lover of art of all genres, also dreamed of bringing favorite pieces of American sculpture to the White House. Along with designer Kaki Hockersmith, Mrs. Clinton and I planned for a series of exhibits in the Jacqueline Kennedy Garden that would include works from public museums in different regions of the country. Since the first exhibit, which included George Segal's *Walking Man* and Alexander Calder's *Five Rudders,* opened in 1994, millions of visitors have walked past the garden, admiring some of this country's contemporary masterpieces. As did Mrs. Kennedy, Mrs. Clinton believes in the power of art to uplift and enhance everyone's life, and the popularity of the exhibits in the Jacqueline Kennedy Garden has proven Mrs. Clinton's enthusiasm contagious.

Congress appropriates funds for the daily operation and maintenance of the White House. However, much necessary refurbishing and all acquisitions have come from the private sector, either through gifts or the proceeds from the White House Historical Association, which now has subsumed the White House Endowment Fund. Mrs. Clinton's vigorous support helped double that fund to more than $25 million, and she has taken an active role in the recent renovations of the Blue Room, the East Room, the Entrance Hall, and the State Dining Room, none of which could have been accomplished without the support of those funds.

I have admired the seriousness with which Mrs. Clinton takes her role as temporary custodian of the White House. As you walk through this national treasure, you will find evidence of her devotion to the arts everywhere you turn—from sculpture in the Jacqueline Kennedy Garden and the refurbished state rooms and acquisitions to the gala performances and events honoring arts and artists that occur regularly on the South Lawn. Moreover, she has worked imaginatively to open the doors of the White House to many more people, not just tourists and visiting dignitaries, but also those who share its magic through their television sets or the Internet.

The pages that follow offer not just a perspective on history, art, and furnishings, but a behind-the-scenes glimpse of how the White House works. From its description of how the thousands of tourists who walk through the public rooms each week are welcomed, to its picture of the military-like precision required to entertain a visiting head of state, *An Invitation to the White House* is an unprecedented opportunity to share in the daily life of the people's house.

Top: The past and the present side by side in the East Room: a portrait of Martha Washington by Eliphalet F. Andrews and a video monitor with a performance by jazz vocalist Sarah Vaughan. Bottom: Mrs. Clinton and J. Carter Brown, director emeritus of the National Gallery of Art, discuss sculpture in the First Lady's garden.

INTRODUCTION

BY

Carl Sferrazza Anthony

Right: The first couple share a quiet moment in the Blue Room before the 1996 National Governors' Association Annual Dinner.

I RECALL ONE OF MY FIRST conversations with Hillary Clinton, shortly after she became First Lady. As we discussed some of the individuals featured in my two-volume history, *First Ladies,* her reverence for her predecessors and her love of the White House were clear, as was her sense of responsibility for the house and her awareness of the role she was to play.

Many people know Mrs. Clinton for her groundbreaking contributions to the policy arena. Fewer know the mark she has made on the responsibilities of the First Lady, honoring the traditions begun by those before her while bringing new ideas and innovations to the position. Mrs. Clinton has a natural affinity and affection for many of her predecessors; Dolley Madison is a particular favorite, and to hear Mrs. Clinton detail aspects of the legendary hostess's legacy is to see evidence of how an earlier life can reach across the decades to inspire another. The First Lady's description of Dolley Madison could be used to describe Mrs. Clinton herself: "Not only a wonderful hostess but a very skilled diplomat with a tremendous political ear, who could bring people together, have them work together, and then send them out feeling that they were charged with a mission."

Anyone who has been to one of the hundreds of the Clintons' parties can see how seriously Mrs. Clinton takes her role as hostess. To see her circulate through the crowds, pointing out objects of interest, posing for endless snapshots, and putting a reassuring arm around a nervous visitor, is to realize that her love of the house is rivaled only by the joy she gets in sharing it with people from all walks of life. I recall seeing her talking to a circle of guests at an evening celebrating

Below: The President, Mrs. Clinton, teenagers, and their parents are announced into the East Room for the White House Conference on Teenagers, May 2, 2000.

the life of Thomas Jefferson and excitedly leading them to see the new red carpet she had finally managed to have installed in the regal hall between the State Dining Room and the East Room. Afterwards she implored everyone to examine the gold centerpiece that has been in the White House collection since it was bought by James Monroe, and, of course, urged them all to indulge in the trays of desserts on the long table.

Like other First Ladies, Mrs. Clinton has been responsible for overseeing the menu at the White House, and one of her first acts was to reinstate the tradition of serving the finest regional American food. Jefferson insisted on serving fresh seafood from the Chesapeake Bay and locally grown vegetables, while the Coolidges offered many of their native New England specialties to guests: brown bread, cheddar cheese, codfish, and maple cookies. At one State Dinner, Mamie Eisenhower had *pomme de brune* listed on formal menus for dessert, but it was still her favorite Apple Brown Betty from Gettysburg, Pennsylvania. While the last several decades brought a decidedly European flavor to the White House table, Hillary Clinton decided it was time to bring in a top American-trained,

Right: Ann Stock, White House Social Secretary from 1993 to 1997

American-born chef, change the table service from French to American, and use American-grown ingredients whenever possible. The results have been fine indeed.

The furnishings and decorations of the White House are the traditional purview of the First Lady. In this arena,

Above: Mrs. Clinton holds a scheduling meeting with senior staff members Capricia Marshall, Kelly Craighead, Marsha Berry, Patti Solis Doyle, Melanne Verveer, Missy Kincaid, Shirley Sagawa, Anne Donovan, and Ellen McCulloch-Lovell.

Mrs. Clinton has been extraordinarily sensitive to preserving historical detail while modernizing rooms on the State Floor. Consider the Blue Room. In 1961 Mrs. Kennedy used original furniture purchased from France by the Monroes in her cream-and-blue refurbishment. The room, so well used during the next decade, became threadbare by 1972, and Pat Nixon undertook another refurbishment, changing the wall covering and the shade of blue of the draperies, but still maintaining the feel of the previous room. Twenty years later, it again required attention. When it was unveiled by Mrs. Clinton in 1995, the room was a rich sapphire blue that looked good when lighted for television, but still preserved the style and furniture of the Monroe era. Now the room as redone in 1972, 1961, or even 1817 might have been perfectly preserved for generations with glass or red velvet ropes across the door, as in a

Top: President and Mrs. Clinton in a lighthearted moment with Governor and Mrs. Ventura at the 1999 National Governors' Association dinner.

Bottom: The President, Mrs. Clinton, and Social Secretary Ann Stock at the 1996 dinner commemorating the 50th anniversary of the Fulbright Program.

museum, but this is the White House:
Lively parties, Christmas receptions,
solemn ceremonies, receiving lines, seated
dinners, and photo sessions all take place
in the Blue Room. It lives and thus it
evolves. Mrs. Clinton understands this
fine balance perfectly.

The use of the house as a national stage
featuring the best contemporary enter-
tainment also follows a White House cus-
tom: The Kennedys requested that the
American Ballet Theater perform in the
East Room; the Eisenhowers asked Fred
Waring and his Pennsylvanians to sing
after a dinner; and Lyndon and Lady Bird
Johnson had Herb Alpert and the Tijuana
Brass perform for them in the 1960s. The
Clintons have carried on this long-stand-
ing tradition, showcasing performers from
Isaac Stern to Eric Clapton.

Of course, like other first families, the
Clintons have also established new
traditions. While it was the Benjamin
Harrison family that brought the first
Christmas tree to the White House, the
Clintons have opened the holiday season
with acknowledgment of both Jewish and
Muslim holy times. The Tafts used the
lawn for the first known performance of
Shakespeare at the White House, and
other families gave garden parties and

*Above: Two guitar
masters, two unique
styles: Eric Clapton and
B. B. King at the October
23, 1999, VH1 Save the
Music concert.
Right: Yo-Yo Ma is
accompanied by Edgar
Meyer and Mark O'Con-
nor at a State Dinner for
President Eduardo Frei,
of the Republic of Chile,
February 6, 1997.*

State Dinners in the Rose Garden, but the Clintons have found even more creative uses for the lawn as a space for sculpture exhibits, large-scale State Dinners (held in an elegant pavilion specially constructed for the events), picnics and cookouts, and even a carnival. By using this large space for entertaining, the Clintons have enabled large numbers of guests to enjoy the White House inside and out.

It is in furthering this rich tradition of making the White House the people's house that the Clintons have had their greatest impact. What makes the White House so different from the homes and palaces of other world leaders is the life that "the people"—the tourists, the dinner guests, the staff, and the

families—bring to its old walls. Were it not for the people who come to the White House, it would simply be a museum, or a beautiful private estate. What makes the White House so special, so distinctly American, is that everyone—however different, from whatever political party, age, or station in life—can visit.

Since the 19th century, tourists have come to marvel at the paintings of past Presidents, ask the staff what the family eats for dinner, watch the delivery wagons come and go—and even snip a curtain tassel for a souvenir. Gates and doors were flung open to the masses at weekly band concerts on the lawn, at the annual Independence Day reception, and for the Egg Roll on Easter Monday, an event still open to the public today. Although security concerns and costs limited the number of "come one, come all" events as the population grew in the 20th century, the Clintons have worked to keep the doors of the people's house open to a great diversity of Americans. Almost every guest list compiled by Hillary Clinton has included those who never thought they might one day receive an invitation to the White House. At these events, one can always expect to meet remarkable people from all walks of life who came to the attention of the Clintons because of a touching letter they had written or important work they had done in their own communities.

The Clintons have also followed the tradition of using the latest technology to bring the White House to those who cannot visit in person. Rutherford and Lucy Hayes were the first to permit a reporter into the private quarters. The Harrisons first allowed the rooms to be photographed for reprinting in newspapers and books. Harry Truman hosted the first televised tour for the nation. And, in 1993 the Clintons permitted C-SPAN (the cable television station that broadcasts political and historical programming to millions of homes) to cover the large State Dinner they hosted in honor of President Nelson Mandela of South Africa, in order to provide a glimpse of the effort that goes into such an event. Along with White House Social Secretary Ann Stock, Mrs. Clinton guided viewers through the earlier planning stages, showing everything from choosing the menu to the music to the table decorations. She also provided commentary on the political impact of what seem like simply "social" functions. Similarly, the Clintons have made frequent use of satellites to bring

events to viewers around the world, and did the first cybercast events, including White House conferences and lectures by prominent Americans, to make them accessible to viewers at their home computers.

An Invitation to the White House is in keeping with this spirit. This book makes the rooms come alive—one can almost taste the food and hear the music. It is not only informative, but inspiring. My own lifelong interest in the White House was prompted by reading books on the subject. I imagined what the rooms looked like, and what it would be like to attend an event there. A first visit to the White House as a young tourist left me feeling extraordinarily privileged and only deepened my interest in the people's house, sending me back to my books for further study. *An Invitation to the White House* will do the same for generations to come.

The Clinton Blue Room will someday be refurbished. New portraits with new faces will be hung on the walls. Other families will come and go. Whatever the length of their stay, each will leave their own mark on the White House in the centuries to follow. The Clintons certainly have, and the nation can be grateful.

*Top: Pastry Chef Roland Mesnier
Bottom: Flora Bunda, a light but
elegant dessert of lemon sorbet
and flowers made of fresh fruit.*

$\mathcal{P}$RESERVING THE HOUSE FOR HISTORY

Above: Mrs. Clinton with Richard Nylander, a member of the Committee for the Preservation of the White House, and historian William Seale.
Opposite page: Chief Usher Gary Walters displays fabric samples for Mrs. Clinton, designer Kaki Hockersmith, and the Committee in the Blue Room in February 1994.

When I was a little girl, I was fascinated by the White House, and couldn't wait to see it. Finally, the summer I was ten, my family visited our nation's capital. We stood outside the fence along the south side staring at the house that symbolizes America for the world. Years later, whenever I flew into Washington, as the plane swept low over the Potomac, I would strain for a glimpse of its graceful, stately lines. But I didn't go inside until Bill and I were invited by President and Mrs. Carter to attend a dinner honoring the Prime Minister of Canada in 1977.

When Bill was governor of Arkansas we were fortunate to return many times for the annual Governors' Dinners hosted by Presidents Reagan and Bush. I loved dressing up in a formal gown and entering the East Wing, receiving our table cards, and being escorted by a social aide up to the State Floor to be greeted by the President and First Lady.

Nothing, however, could prepare me for the sense of awe I felt when my family arrived at the White House in 1993. Wherever we looked there was something—a clock, a chandelier, a painting, a chair—that told a story about the people and events that have shaped our country's history. In the hallways, we saw Presidents and First Ladies peering down from their official portraits. Outside our bedroom windows, we saw the grand magnolia planted by Andrew Jackson, which blooms magnificently in the spring. I imagined Abraham Lincoln working on the Emancipation Proclamation in what is now known as the Lincoln Bedroom, and Franklin Roosevelt holding his fireside chats from the Diplomatic Reception Room.

It takes a lot of work to keep any house up and running. That's especially true for the White House, which, having just celebrated its 200th anniversary as the President's home, is now the oldest official residence of a head of state anywhere in the world. Imagine the wear and tear on a place that welcomes up to 30,000 guests a week and the care it takes to protect and preserve 132 different rooms, and many priceless American artifacts.

Early in the administration, Bill and I would wake up every morning not to an alarm clock, but to the sounds of workers on scaffolding outside our windows. They were part of a crew of masons, painters, and carpenters who were renovating the exterior of the White House, including removing some 40 coats of paint and repairing the original stone.

Not long after we arrived we were informed that the heating and air conditioning system needed to be overhauled. This was its first major update since the Truman administration, when an engineering survey reported that the White House was "standing up purely from habit." President Truman had to relocate to Blair House for three and a half years while the entire interior of the house was gutted and restored.

Like every presidential family that came before us, we know that we are temporary custodians of a national museum and that we have the responsibility to pass it on to future generations.

I read about past renovations and knew that I would have to make some difficult choices to preserve the unique history and character of the house. I wanted to be actively involved on all fronts—in communicating to the public why restoring the White House is so important; in working with experts to choose and implement the appropriate designs, styles, fixtures, and colors; and in raising the funds to make it possible.

We had to prioritize, and the Blue Room seemed to need the most attention. It gets a lot of sunlight, which is wonderful, especially when Bill and I are greeting guests there. However, it also means that the fabric tends to fade. When we first moved in, the once vibrant blue draperies and upholstery had faded to a pale aqua. We knew we had to pick a perfect tone of blue, one that would withstand the light and also appropriately reflect the room and its history.

For two years, I met with a group of historians, curators, and designers from the Committee for the Preservation of the White House to review fabric samples and textures. We agreed to continue the French Empire style selected by President and Mrs. Monroe in 1817, when the house was rebuilt and refurnished after the British soldiers burned it in 1814. After committee members Kaki Hockersmith, Wendy Cooper, Richard Nylander, and Betty Monkman researched wallpaper designs from that period, we selected an early-19th-century French design for the wallpaper and borders and a deep sapphire blue and gold for the draperies and to reupholster the original furniture.

I remember how vibrant this new blue color looked when I first walked into the room. But, as White House historian Bill

Seale and I looked around, something was still not quite right. Finally, our eyes settled on the trompe l'oeil bordering the ceiling. We wanted it to have more of a draped look. So, I suggested taking a small sample of the wallpaper and cutting a moon-shaped sliver out of it. It worked. We did the same thing around the entire border, which provided the finishing touch.

When it was time to focus on the State Dining Room, I wanted to combine elements from past renovations with the style and decor appropriate for the 50,000 guests who come there for State Dinners and receptions each year. When they walk in now, guests see new silk brocade draperies, reproduced from a 1901 pattern, and a beautiful new carpet with wide decorative borders and a field pattern of flowers and acorns, which were popular during the Colonial Revival period when Theodore Roosevelt was President. If he were to come back for a visit today, he

might be disappointed to find that his 11 big game heads no longer grace the walls. He would however notice that the committee and I have preserved and restored many of his furnishings. We cleaned the chandelier and recovered the Queen Anne—style mahogany chairs. We stripped down the three eagle-pedestal console tables to their original wood finish. The wall sconces, once covered by a matte finish, have now been restored to their true gold color.

And we've been able to do that all around the house. In fact, one day I was riding in the President's elevator, and I noticed a spot underneath the faux covering that looked like it could be the original wood. I took my fingernail and flicked part of it away. Sure enough, there was wood underneath that I wanted to uncover. Workmen chipped away the covering and, with toothbrushes, restored the panelling to its original burnished sheen.

Above left: Mrs. Clinton, Kaki Hockersmith, and art historian William Kloss at a March 3,1997, meeting of the Committee for the Preservation of the White House. Above right: Mrs. Clinton and Kaki Hockersmith look at carpet samples for the Cross Hall in August 1995.

As we made these kinds of decisions about the state rooms, I thought not only about the histories of the rooms, but also about how they are used now, and how they may be used in the future. That was particularly important when it came to the Cross Hall, the backdrop for some of the most powerful images the American people see of their President.

The President takes a long walk down the carpet into the East Room several times a month—to enter a press conference, a bill signing, or a ceremonial event, often escorted by a foreign leader. Because most Americans will only see this picture on television, how it looks on camera is just as important as how it looks in person. So when Kaki Hockersmith and I were examining carpet and fabric designs for this area, we looked at samples under natural light as well as bright television lights.

Other spaces are in the spotlight less often, but deserve no less care. The Map Room, on the ground floor, is where Prime Minister Winston Churchill and President Franklin Roosevelt sat poring over military maps, charting the destiny of nations and people during World War II. When my family arrived at the White House, we learned this room was used very little. To me, this small space was a gem of a room

Above: The Grand Staircase with new carpet and draperies. The border design, by Kaki Hockersmith, echoes the design of the ironwork in the lower section of the railing.

holding the echoes of two brilliant leaders whose courage and voices will never be forgotten.

I asked that the Map Room be repainted and refurnished so that the room and its memories could come alive again. I wondered what the room had looked like when President Roosevelt used it and whether there were any maps available from that time. Unfortunately, because the room had been top secret—off-limits even to Mrs. Roosevelt—there were few records to help us. Finally, my curiosity led me to George Elsey, who had been a young lieutenant assigned to President Roosevelt. He remembered the room and graciously described it to William Gemmell, a White House calligrapher, who used the description to draw a sketch that is displayed in the Map Room today. Mr. Elsey had also kept the last map prepared for President Roosevelt before the President died at Warm Springs, Georgia. The map, showing Allied troop movements in Europe, now hangs over the fireplace.

This room is central to our life at the White House. Bill and I use it for meetings and entertaining small groups, and we love retelling its history. Once we held a small dinner there for an old friend. He had been part of the American military's march through Europe. He had tears in his eyes as he looked at the map, retracing his footsteps a half-century later.

We've also renovated rooms in the private quarters: the Lincoln Sitting Room; the President's Dining Room, where our family, like every first family since 1961, enjoy private meals together; and the Treaty Room. When you are the President of the United States, you always bring your work home; Bill brings his to the Treaty Room. Located on the second floor of the house, it is named for the historic documents signed on the table in it, including the Peace Protocol ending the Spanish-American War, the Arms Limitation Treaty with the Soviet Union (SALT). Early in 1993, when Kaki and I first began making plans for the President's office in the residence, Bill made it very clear that he wanted to be closely involved in the project.

For his desk, he selected the eight-drawer walnut conference table first used by President Grant and his Cabinet in this room. During our time, this table was moved to the South Lawn and the East Room for signing agreements between Israel and the Palestinians in 1993, Israel and Jordan in 1994, and the Wye Accord in 1997. Bill chose the deep red and blue colors used throughout the room. And he has filled it with

Top: A French ornamental clock, circa 1785, adorns the mantel in the Family Dining Room.
Bottom: Drawer pulls on a sideboard in the Family Dining Room bear the likeness of George Washington.

Left: The State Dining Room during Theodore Roosevelt's administration. Note the mounted animal heads.
Below: The Joint High Commissioners dine in high style in the State Dining Room in March 1871.

Opposite page: The refurbishing of the State Dining Room, including carpet, draperies, chairs, and lighting fixtures, was completed in 1999.

personal items, including his golf putter collection, a stereo, CDs, and books in bookcases that cover the walls from floor to ceiling. In fact, Bill actually worked with the carpenters to design these bookshelves himself so they would fit with the antique furnishings as well as hold a large number of his books, which range from volumes of Shakespeare to books on golf.

When it came time to focus on the Lincoln Sitting Room, we wanted to fill it with everything we could find from that period. We brought items from storage and from all over the house. At one point, Bill and I found ourselves standing in the East Sitting Hall sorting through possible items for the room. We found, for example, a program from Lincoln's first Inaugural Ball, two chairs the Lincolns had given as a wedding present, and a late-19th-century telephone that still works—all of which are now in the Lincoln Sitting Room.

Every first family has faced the challenge of how to pay for the upkeep of the house. In the 19th century, they often sold old furniture to pay for the new. For example,

some Monroe Blue Room gilded furniture was sold in 1860 to buy pieces in the Victorian style. Today Congress funds the maintenance of the house. But, until recently, families had to make a special appeal for private donations every time they needed to carry out a renovation in the state rooms or make an acquisition.

It wasn't until 1961, at the urging of Jacqueline Kennedy, that anyone thought about preserving the rooms and furnishings in the same way we do in other museums. Her idea was to create a White House Historical Association, which has since increased appreciation for the house while raising funds for acquisitions and renovations of the public rooms. She also hired the first White House curator and established an informal advisory committee on preservation, innovations later formalized by President Johnson.

In 1979 Rosalynn Carter had the idea for a permanent endowment for the White House. Ten years later, Barbara Bush created the White House Endowment Fund to provide permanent support for the house's fine art, furnishings, and renova-

Right: The historic Treaty Room is traditionally used as an office and a sitting room by the President.

tions. I was happy to take responsibility for the fund when we arrived, and could not have been more pleased when, in 1998, thanks to the help of many generous people, we not only met but exceeded the goal of raising $25 million for the endowment. What this means, I hope, is that none of my successors will ever be burdened by the responsibility of raising money for the house. They will be able to pay for all their renovations and restorations solely off the interest from this fund. I can't think of a better gift to the future.

When I walk through the house today, it is hard to imagine what Abigail Adams encountered when she arrived here at the turn of the 19th century. There was no running water and little heat, and she had to hang the presidential wash in the East Room to dry. Nevertheless, like every other first family, she and President Adams understood that they were stewards, not owners, of the people's house.

Because so many have understood their role in caring for the White House these past two centuries, it still stands as the most powerful symbol of our country's history.

This is the history that fascinated me as a young girl and inspires me every day as I walk the hallways and work to honor the dreams and contributions of all those who came before. This is the living history of America that each of us has a responsibility to preserve, protect, and ultimately pass on to future generations.

Above left: President and Mrs. Clinton are joined by President and Mrs. Carter, President Bush, and President and Mrs. Ford for the signing of the North Atlantic Free Trade Agreement, September 13, 1993.
Above right: President Clinton meeting with former Presidents Ford, Carter, and Bush in the Treaty Room, September 13, 1993. The painting is The Signing of the Peace Protocol between Spain and the United States, August 12, 1898, *by Theobald Chartran.*

MAKING THIS HOUSE A HOME

*Above: The President, Socks, nephew
Tyler Clinton, and Buddy play catch
on the White House lawn.*

Top: Chelsea talks on the phone while her dad appears on television on the day of his second inauguration. Bottom: Decorations for a party celebrating Chelsea's graduation from high school, June 7, 1997.

Before we arrived at the White House, there hadn't been a pre-teen daughter in the residence since Amy Carter. Chelsea, then just twelve years old, had moved away from the only home she had ever known, the governor's residence in Little Rock, Arkansas. Although we had little doubt that Chelsea would make many new friends and enjoy her life in Washington, D.C., we knew that in the beginning it would be a tough transition for all of us. We wanted her to have warm, loving spaces where she could curl up with a book, watch television, sit on the floor, listen to music, study quietly, challenge (and beat) her dad in a game of cards, or have good times with friends. We wanted the White House to be a place that Chelsea—and our entire family—could truly call home.

Above: The President's music room was created as a Christmas surprise.
Below: On a chair in the family living room rests a needlepoint pillow of the cover of Mrs. Clinton's bestselling book, It Takes a Village. It was a gift from First Lady volunteer Phyllis Fineshriber.

When I look back at the last eight years, I think of the pizza parties Chelsea threw for her friends in the State Dining Room. I think of her classmates from Stanford who stayed in our home during holiday breaks and of the late nights our daughter and her friends spent camped out across the third floor for their famous "Bunking Parties." During these celebrated events, it was not uncommon to hear this group of teenage girls giggling as they slid down the ramp that connects the third floor to the solarium.

It is, in fact, that sun-filled solarium, packed with overstuffed blue-and-white floral print sofas, that has been the all-purpose room for our daughter through

all these years as she has gone from pre-teen to teenager to college student.

Called a "sky parlor" by Mrs. Coolidge and used as a schoolroom for Caroline Kennedy, the solarium is our chief activity room. It is a place where we can really hang out, especially when our two nephews are on the loose and in need of lots of floor space. The walls that line the ramp showcase a photographic history of the life and times of the Rodhams and the Clintons, each one a precious piece of our family's story. Some of my favorites? A family portrait taken when Chelsea was a year old; a beautiful watercolor sketch of Bill's mother; a picture of Chelsea and her father dancing at his last inauguration; Bill and I relaxing in a hammock at a friend's house in Arkansas. I love taking a walk up that ramp at dusk when the light is falling just so on the pictures of the relatives and friends who are so much a part of our lives.

There is always a place in every house where families tend to gather—usually it's the place where food can be found. Our family is no different. But when we arrived at the White House, there was no family kitchen in our living quarters. Our first official act was to convert what had been a chef's kitchen off the President's

Right: The east end of the second-floor corridor in the private quarters. On the wall above the piano hangs Untitled XXXIX *by Willem de Kooning, on loan from the de Kooning estate. Next to it is* Group in Crinolines [Reifrockgesellschaft] *by Vasily Kandinsky, on loan from the Solomon R. Guggenheim Museum. The glass bowl in the foreground is* Cobalt Macchia with Green Lip Wrap *by Dale Chihuly.*

Above: The President's Dining Room was redecorated in 1997. The moire silk fabric is hung on special supports to protect the historic wallpaper underneath. The painting above the fireplace is Marjorie and Little Edmund, *by Edmund Tarbell, 1928. It is on loan from the National Museum of American Art, Smithsonian Institution.*

Dining Room into a livable kitchen. Our kitchen is the place where Bill and I eat dinner together or have a glass of champagne after an event, or raid the refrigerator for leftovers when we come home late after attending a dinner at which we found no time to eat! It's also the place Chelsea meets her father and me for breakfast and dinner when she's home. I can also find Bill and the butlers watching football or basketball games there.

When it is actually time to sit down with larger groups of family, friends, staff members, or special guests for dinner, conversation, and, of course, political debate, we eat in the President's Dining Room next door to our second-floor kitchen. Before the Kennedy administration, most families were served their meals in the Family Dining Room on the

state floor. First Lady Jacqueline Kennedy asked for a dining room in the residence so that her young children could stay in the family's home for their meals. Before it was the President's Dining Room it was used as a bedroom for Presidents Cleveland and McKinley. One medical operation is even known to have taken place in this room— an appendectomy on Alice Roosevelt Longworth. Margaret Truman used it for her sitting room and kept her piano there. One of the reasons President Truman decided to renovate the whole house was because of his fear that the piano might fall through the floor.

When we want to relax with our family and friends outside, we often go to the swimming pool, which was constructed by President Ford. He once conducted a press conference from the pool, bathing suit and all. The pool is located near the Oval

Above left: The President uses the Treaty Room as an office. Furnished with objects that are rich in history, it is also full of items of personal significance. Above right: The West Sitting Hall where Mrs. Clinton loves to sit. Below: Gorgeous bouquets of flowers are always on display in both the public and private rooms of the White House.

Above: Mrs. Clinton at home in the West Sitting Hall. Right: The photo gallery on the ramp to the solarium in the residence.

Office, discreetly tucked away behind a row of greenery and trees. One of our favorite times there was the poolside barbecue and birthday celebration I held for the President and Tipper Gore, who share the same birthday, August 19. Both of our families had a great time together trading stories, laughing, and eating way too much good food—just like any Americans at a barbecue on a lazy afternoon.

This is actually the second pool constructed at the White House. The first was an indoor pool built during Franklin Roosevelt's administration, partly financed by contributions from school children. In 1969, it was covered over to provide a place for White House reporters to work. It is now the press briefing room, which you often see on television when the president or press secretary briefs reporters.

The West Sitting Hall on the second floor of the White House is essentially our family living room. Its large Palladian window overlooks the Rose Garden and the Oval Office. Books we are currently reading are stacked on the coffee table, along with a pad and pen for my ever-expanding "to do" list. (In fact, "to do" lists seem to spontaneously appear on pads all over the

house.) This is where I conduct much of my day-to-day business, from making phone calls to assembling care packages for Chelsea while she's so far away at Stanford. Each of us makes a beeline to the Sitting Hall at the end of each day to talk about our daily activities, discuss family business, compare calendars, and make plans. It is also our family staging area, the room where we get ready to go on a trip, compose ourselves before heading to the State Floor for a White House event, or say good-night to Chelsea and her friends before they go out for the evening. The room is a high-traffic area but there are moments of peace to be found here too. During the afternoon and early evening, sunlight floods through the grand fan window that dominates this lovely spot, making it a comfortable place to read and reflect.

Everyone knows about the President's love of music, but no one knows better than I about the President's love of musical "stuff." One year, for a Christmas surprise, I got together with Kaki Hockersmith, my friend and interior designer, who has helped us decorate our private quarters as well as the state rooms, to create a music room for my husband. We decided to convert a small room with a charming staircase and balcony, previously used as a family sitting room, into Bill's music room. Now his saxophone collection, old record albums, photographs of favorite

Above: Strawberry shortcake, Chef Mesnier style, was served at Maggie's shower.

Above: Mrs. Clinton tries her hand at the harp at a Wellesley reunion at the White House, February 3, 1995.

Above: The 1996 Fourth of July celebration on the White House roof, one of the best places to view the fireworks.

Right: At the September 23, 1996, birthday party for Kevin O'Keefe, a friend of the Clintons, Social Secretary Ann Stock consults with butler Jim Selmon.

musicians, stacks of sheet music, and his ever-expanding CD collection have found a home.

I have my favorite things too. My personal treasures have accumulated over a lifetime, and mark important moments from my life in Washington. One such keepsake is a needlepoint pillow replica of the cover of my book, *It Takes a Village,* crafted by Phyllis Fineschriber, a long-time volunteer in the Office of the First Lady.

One of the privileges of living in the White House is being surrounded by great art. I have been deeply honored to participate in the selection of art for the public venues of the White House, but it has been an absolute delight to choose the art that our family lives with every day. As I have said previously, in addition to dis-

playing the art from the White House collection, I've also borrowed works from outside collections. Bill and I have a great time (and a few disagreements!) deciding where the pieces should be placed. I selected the abstract *Untitled XXXIX* from Willem de Kooning's personal collection to place over the piano and command the Center Hall alongside Vasily Kandinsky's *Group in Crinolines* from the Solomon R. Guggenheim Museum. From the White House collection I chose Paul Cézanne's *Mont Sainte Victoire and Hamlet, Near Gardanne* to hang above the mantel in the Yellow Oval Room and Claude Monet's *Morning on the Seine, Good Weather* to hang directly in front of my favorite chair in the West Sitting Hall. On the third floor, our overnight guests can enjoy a Rothko, a Peale, and a Prendergast.

Above left: Mrs. Clinton greets her mother and father, January 30, 1993. Above right: The President says a few words before the June 6, 1995, screening of Apollo 13. *Director Ron Howard stands at right; Lew and Edie Wasserman watch from the front row.*

Above left: A surprise candlelit celebration for Mrs. Clinton's 50th birthday, held in the State Dining Room in October 1997.
Above right: Mrs. Clinton goes country for her 48th birthday in 1995.
Right: The President and Chelsea share a dance at Mrs. Clinton's fifties-theme birthday party in 1994.

One of our greatest joys is sharing the experience of living in the White House with our family, friends, and supporters. They come not as official visitors, but as personal guests to our home. The President has been known to give tours of the house as late as 2 a.m. We have holiday sing-alongs around the piano. Secretary of Health and Human Services Donna Shalala and other Cabinet secretaries, staff members, and guests are often found out on the tennis court on the South Lawn. Our Super Bowl parties boast chili, nachos, hamburgers, and often food from the home states of the competing teams. The doors to the room are left open so people can yell at the screens when things heat up.

We are also all big movie fans. So whenever we have a free evening, watching a movie is high on our list of things to do. President Franklin Roosevelt had a small movie theater constructed in the White House to view popular films of the day. The theater, refurbished to its current state during the Reagan administration, seats 47 comfortably and over 70 when we have to accommodate unexpected crowds. The White House movie theater was reportedly used by President Eisenhower to see as many as 100 movies a year during his time in office. Although we cannot quite top that number, we do see our fair share. Often it is just the three of us or Bill and me. Other times we fill the room with guests, sometimes including the actors who appear in the film. One favorite movie night was the preview of *Apollo 13* with John Glenn, director Ron Howard, and the three stars of that movie: Tom Hanks, Kevin Bacon, and Gary Sinese.

We've also celebrated many milestones for our friends in the house. For example, we were all thrilled when my Chief of Staff Maggie Williams set a date to wed Bill Barrett. One brilliant sunny afternoon, Maggie's friends and family, led by her redoubtable mother, Erma, gathered in the Yellow Oval Room to tell stories and open countless presents. The "women only" party was crashed by the President, who kidded and toasted Maggie until she blushed.

Above: The President and Mrs. Clinton dressed as James and Dolley Madison at a surprise costume birthday party for Mrs. Clinton in 1993.

Shortly after we moved into the White House, we celebrated the engagement of James Carville and Mary Matalin with a grand reception. James had been one of the President's closest campaign advisors and Mary had been a key political advisor in President Bush's campaign inner circle. The entire Carville clan came up from Louisiana, including James's mother, an American original whom he fondly calls "Miss Nippy," and whom we all love.

The tradition of celebrating weddings at the White House is a very old one. Dolley Madison's sister, Lucy Payne Washington, and Supreme Court Justice Thomas Todd were the first couple to be married in the White House in 1812. The first child of a President to be married in the White House was Maria Monroe, the daughter of President James Monroe, in 1820. And the first and only President to be married in the White House was President Grover Cleveland, who wed his bride, the 21-year-old beauty Frances Folsom, in 1886. Tricia Nixon and Edward Cox were the first couple to be wed in an outside setting in the Rose Garden at the White House.

As a general rule, Bill, Chelsea, and I initiate most of the personal entertaining done at the White House. We decide what movies to watch and whom to invite for our Fourth of July rooftop party. We exchange ideas about guests and music for the birthday parties of family, friends, and staff. Bill and I both invited our high school classes to the White House for reunions and hosted the 25th and 30th reunions of our alma maters—Wellesley and Georgetown. We both enjoy planning how to share this extraordinary experience with as many people as possible, but sometimes the tables get turned and a party gets planned without us.

That is what happened in 1993 when my staff and friends decided to surprise me with a costume party for my birthday, October 26. I came home to the White

Above: Staff surprised President Clinton with a western-theme party for his 49th birthday in 1995.
Right: Chief of Staff Leon Panetta with Deputy Chiefs of Staff Harold Ickes and Erskine Bowles at the President's birthday party on the South Lawn.

House after a long day of events and found the house completely dark. I could not imagine what had happened. But I soon found out as one of my staff members silently led me up in the elevator to my bedroom, where a costume and black wig awaited me. Within moments I was transformed into Dolley Madison.

The next year I was surprised again when I was handed a poodle skirt! Descending the stairs to the Grand Foyer, I found a 1950s-style living room, complete with plastic-covered couches and small black-and-white television sets. The foyer was filled with singing and dancing well-wishers, many of them costumed to look like me or characters from *Happy Days* or *Grease*. My husband played his part as well, clad in black leather jacket and jeans. I relived my high school years, jitterbugging the night away.

I'm not the only one who has enjoyed a surprise birthday celebration. When Bill turned 49, the staff organized a western-theme party (in honor of our upcoming trip to Jackson Hole, Wyoming), complete with horses on the South Lawn.

With memories like these, I know that when the three of us wave good-bye to the White House, we will miss not only the history of the people's house, but the warmth of the family home we created within it.

Above: Chelsea shows her mother her attire on their way to the second Inaugural Ceremony and festivities. Right: President and Mrs. Clinton in the President's Elevator, on their way to the second Inaugural Ball, 1997.

Above: National Park Service gardeners Stanley Dufrane and Tom Greer bringing in the spring plantings.

Right: Prime Minister Rabin, President Mubarak, King Hussein, President Clinton, and Chairman Arafat in the Red Room of the White House minutes before the signing of the historic September 28, 1995, Peace Accords.

Behind the Scenes

Above: A calligrapher pens the President's place card for the United Kingdom Official Dinner.

When Bill, Chelsea, and I arrived at our new home on Inauguration Day 1993, waiting to greet us were some of the 90 men and women whose tireless efforts behind the scenes make the White House come alive in all its roles—as a home for each first family, as the center of the American presidency, and as the host to a million and a half visitors a year.

At first, when my family walked through the halls, the residence staff would follow tradition and duck into the doorways out of respect for our privacy. Now they have come to feel like family. They clip articles they think we might be interested in and leave them between the toaster and television in the kitchen. We celebrate good news together, rejoicing when Mary Arnold, the second-floor maid, brought in her new grandbaby or when George Hannie was promoted from butler to maître d', becoming the supervisor of the food and beverage service for all guests.

Sadly, back in 1999, we lost a member of this extended family when Johnny Muffler passed away. His father-in-law was a chauffeur at the White House, and Johnny first arrived here in 1945 to work as an electrician. He stayed over 50 years—the longest serving employee ever. I loved seeing Johnny walking through the halls in his last years, carefully winding every antique clock. We would stop to talk about his family, especially his wife and son, Rick, who has worked in the calligraphy office for 16 years, carrying on his family's proud legacy.

It is not unusual, as in Johnny's case, for a member of the staff, or indeed an entire family, to serve many different Presidents. Other White House staff, like the press secretaries, speech writers, and policy advisers, are political appointees who come and go with each administration. But the residence staff are government employees who serve without regard to politics. Barbara Bush tells the story of one of the butlers who gently reminded her, "Presidents come and go. Butlers stay."

In fact, Gary Walters, who has been the chief usher since 1986, is only the eighth chief usher in the entire history of the White House. Ike Hoover, who stayed 42 years and served 10 Presidents, holds the record for the longest service. The chief usher, a title borrowed from the British and used since the 19th century to describe the executive manager of the

White House, supervises all of the residence staff—from the florists, chefs, kitchen employees, ushers, and butlers who help to welcome visitors to the electricians, carpenters, plumbers, painters, engineers, and housekeepers who keep this old house in tip-top shape.

On our first day, Gary welcomed us to the house, just as each chief usher has done with each first family. We then faced the daunting task of putting into place all the paintings, furniture, and carpets—both those that we brought from Arkansas and those from the extensive White House collection—so we could

Above: Social Secretary Ann Stock and Deputy Social Secretary Ann McCoy peruse the calendar of events.

begin turning the house into our home. That process, I'm forced to confess, took us more than a year!

Gary also gave us an orientation manual, which listed potential upcoming events as well as job descriptions of key staff. Visitors to the White House may never meet these dedicated people, but much of what they experience there is a result of the staffs' dedicated efforts. When guests see an artist performing onstage in the East Room, it is because of the staff in the operations office who moved the antique furniture, built the staging, and made sure the lights went up. And when visitors admire the beautiful 18 acres of grounds, they have the National Park Service employees to thank. Park Service staff mows the lawns, trims the shrubbery, cares for the stately trees, and tends the Rose Garden, which is filled not only with many varieties and colors of roses, but also countless other seasonal flowers. National Park Service employees do all of this under the watchful eyes of Buddy and Socks, and under the direction of Dale Haney and Irv Williams, who worked with Mrs. Paul "Bunny" Mellon to design the Rose Garden for President Kennedy.

When guests attend a formal dinner, they see beautiful flower arrangements created

Above: The First Lady's place setting for a luncheon with Queen Noor of Jordan in 1993. Above right: Florist Wendy Elsasser, Social Secretary Capricia Penavic Marshall, Chief Floral Designer Nancy Clarke, Chief Usher Gary Walters, and Mrs. Clinton review sample table settings in May 1998.

by Chief Floral Designer Nancy Clarke and her staff. The day starts the same for Nancy every morning. She walks through all the rooms on the state floor, checking on the fresh flower arrangements, replacing wilted flowers, adding water, and recycling flowers to make them last as long as possible.

Sometimes when on a trip overseas, I'll have pictures taken of the flower arrangements that our hosts use to share with Nancy. We've tried many different styles, sometimes changing arrangements at the very last minute! As we prepared for the millennium celebration dinner, for exam-

ple, Nancy created beautiful centerpieces of white orchids. But somehow they didn't look quite festive enough for the party that marked the end of an entire century and millennium. So, in the final hours, we added greenery and sparkling silver ornaments to the orchid arrangements, experimenting until we settled upon the green, silver, and white centerpieces that lit up the tables that evening.

It's amazing to think about how much entertaining at the White House has changed. In the early administrations, the invitations were handwritten, one by one,

Left: Part-time
butler Milton
Rowe polishes
glasses before
a luncheon
with governors'
spouses in the
Yellow Oval
Room, February
5, 1996.

by the First Lady and her friends. Fortunately for me and my friends, the White
House now has three calligraphers on staff.

John and Abigail Adams brought only two
servants and held just a half dozen receptions during their short tenure in the
White House. Thomas Jefferson, on the
other hand, set a different tone. Recogniz-
ing the political value of entertaining, he
hosted an informal dinner for a dozen
guests almost every night, spending his
own money lavishly on wine, food, and
staff. On more formal occasions, Jefferson,
who was a widower, called on Dolley
Madison to serve as hostess.

When Dolley Madison became First Lady,
an invitation to the White House became
even more desirable. There was one
dinner though, scheduled for August 24,
1814, that proved to be an utter failure.
The food was prepared. The tables were
all set for President Madison, who was
with his officers fighting the invading
British forces during the War of 1812. But,
it was the British soldiers, not her invited
guests, who sat down and enjoyed the
meal before setting the house and large
piles of its furniture on fire!

Today, the White House kitchen feeds as
many as 2,000 dinner and reception

guests a month, and even more during the holidays. Early White House menus offered "cabbage pudding," "gooseberry fool," fried oysters, and Abigail Adams's "Fourth of July Peas," all American favorites. Later, White House menus took a turn toward our Revolutionary War allies in France, with the hiring of French-trained chefs. When we moved into the White House, I thought the time had come for America's house to once again feature the best of American food.

I scheduled interviews with five extraordinary chefs, all of whom prepared meals for the occasion. One of them, Walter Scheib, a Maryland native and executive chef at The Greenbrier in West Virginia, had studied at the Culinary Institute of America in Hyde Park, New York, and had practiced his craft at some of our nation's greatest hotels. He described the meal he prepared in incredible detail and spoke passionately about why he wanted to showcase thoroughly American cuisine at the White House. And he has.

Since being hired in 1994, Walter has brought some of the finest foods from our country's farms, fields, rivers, and ranches to the White House table. He has visited farmers' markets in search of the freshest

fruits and vegetables, and, even closer to home, he has served up the tomatoes, peppers, squashes, and herbs from the vegetable garden I started on the roof. Even when I am on the second floor, I can smell the hints of what Walter is preparing downstairs with his three assistants—especially before a big dinner. He has also been a teacher, showing me how to combine flavors in new and different ways.

I remember the tender buffalo that Walter served at the NATO dinner, as he emphasized that nothing was more American than buffalo. He finds the most creative and visual ways to serve everything from American caviar to Colorado lamb. And he has helped us make the change from French service to American service, where each course is prearranged on individual plates in the kitchen, which saves both time and mishaps at the tables. I decided to change the form of service when two of our older guests in one week dropped food in their laps trying to serve themselves from the platter held over their left shoulders!

While Walter represents the best in American cooking, Pastry Chef Roland Mesnier is, down to his accent, decidedly French. He is the first pastry chef working

Above: Members of the Marine Band waiting to play at the State Dinner for President Kim Dae-Jung of the Republic of Korea, July 27, 1995.

Right: The President shares a moment of levity with Missy Kincaid, Deputy Social Secretary Sharon Kennedy, Social Aide Maj Jon Roop, Capricia Marshall, and Deputy Social Secretary Kim Widdess after the 1999 Friends of Art and Preservation in Embassies (FAPE) dinner.

in America to receive France's prestigious Pastry Chef of the Year award and now serves as the honorary president of the World Cup of Pastry. Roland was only 14 when his career began as an apprentice. Years later, it took only one interview for Rosalynn Carter to offer him the job at the White House—a testament to his extraordinary talent. Roland's desserts aren't simply baked; they're designed, sculpted, molded, spun, or crafted, creatively combining textures and tastes. Fortunately, or unfortunately, for me, he also happens to make one of my very favorite desserts in the world, mocha mousse cake. When it appears, and then quickly disappears, I'll call Roland, laughing and pleading, "Please don't ever do it again!"

Like every talented craftsman or artist, Roland spends as much time researching his assignment as he does creating it.

Left: Mrs. Clinton takes a moment to freshen up in the Blue Room before she and the President are announced into the State Dining Room for the February 4, 1996, National Governors' Association dinner.

Left: Butlers Smiley Saint-Aubin, Buddy Carter, and James Ramsey, and Maître d' George Hannie confer in the second floor corridor before a June 18, 1998, luncheon.

Below: Pastry Chef Roland Mesnier reviews a dessert before serving. New Year's Day 1998—Chef John Moeller, Executive Chef Walter Scheib, Chef Christeta Comerford, and George Hannie are also at work.

Long before a State Dinner, he calls the embassy for ideas about the preferences of our honored guests and then takes a trip to the library to get even more information.

When Prime Minister Romano Prodi of Italy and his wife visited in May 1998, Roland learned that the Prime Minister's hometown of Bologna is the site of two very special towers, which are as impor-tant to the Bolognese as the famous lean-ing tower is to those from Pisa. Roland created "A Tribute to Bologna," a replica of one of the towers crafted from peach cake, chestnut ice cream parfait, and chocolate caramel sauce. It was a topic of conversa-tion all night. In this case, the framework was just as important as the final product. As Roland explained, "We don't want dessert falling on anyone's lap."

In entertaining, we have tried to use every corner of the White House and its grounds. When we are in town, it is not unusual for Bill and me, between the two of us, to host an award ceremony in the East Room, a meeting in the Map Room, a reception in the Yellow Oval Room, and a dinner on the South Lawn underneath a huge white pavilion. Every last detail of these White House events is overseen by the social secretary, who is appointed by the President, and her staff and volunteers in the Social Office.

I have been very well served by Social Secretaries Ann Stock and Capricia Penavic Marshall, both of whom I met before my family moved into the White House. I first interviewed Ann, a vice president at Bloomingdale's, at Blair House right after the election because I wanted to start working immediately to shape the upcoming social calendar. Capricia, who took over when Ann left in 1997, started as my personal assistant out of law school in 1992. At 35, she is, I believe, one of the youngest social secretaries ever, and probably the first to have a baby during her tenure.

It is not unusual for me to begin meeting with the social secretary months before an important event to start drawing up guest lists, choosing the proper venue, planning the entertainment, reviewing menus, and picking out table settings.

As the date gets closer, the entire Social Office swings into full gear. No gesture is overlooked—from hand-lettering invitations, place cards, and menus to arranging seating charts and working with members of the military staff and the music ensembles to welcome guests as they arrive.

Above: Chef Christeta Comerford, assistant Leland Atckinson, and George Hannie in the family kitchen, plating dishes for a meal that will be served in the President's Dining Room, July 14, 1998.

Bill and I often take our visitors on tours of the house, showing them the beautiful art and antiques that grace every room. I always make a point to show them the breathtaking fourteen-foot mirrored, gilded bronze plateau centerpiece on the table in the State Dining Room. It features the figures of Bacchus and Bacchantes and was chosen by President and Mrs. James Monroe. When we first moved in, we sat many an hour listening

Above: Part-time chefs
Oscar Flores and
Clarence Lipford work
swiftly while butlers
stand by.
Right: Social Secretary
Capricia Marshall directs
the flow of activities.

to members of the Curator's Office, then headed by Rex Scouten, tell great stories about these artifacts and the roles that they played in our nation's history.

The Curator's Office is now led by Betty Monkman, an historian who has been in the office since the Johnson administration. She and her staff research, document, interpret, and care for the house and its furnishings, including the extraordinary collection of White House china, approximately 500 works of fine art, thousands of decorative arts objects, and the handwritten copy of the Gettysburg Address that resides in the Lincoln Bedroom. And the Curator's Office itself is a piece of history. It used to be the White House kitchen, and you can still see the place where pots hung over the open fire.

Though the focus in this chapter is on the staff members who ensure that the house and its events run smoothly, there are hundreds of other men and women who support the Executive Office of the President throughout the complex, which includes not only the East Wing, residence, and West Wing, but also the Eisenhower Executive Office Building, the New Executive Office Building, 750 17th Street,

Opposite page: Mrs. Clinton with some of the many men and women who work behind the scenes and in the public eye to make the events at the White House come to life.

Above (from left to right): Butlers Buddy Carter, Ricardo Sanvictores, Maître d' George Hannie, and butler Smiley Saint-Aubin. Together they have put in 66 years of service to the White House.

also by the White House photographers, whose pictures grace many of these pages. If you walk through the ground floor of the West Wing, where the Photography Office is located, you can see all the new photographs of our most recent events and trips. The White House photographers—Sharon Farmer, Bob McNeely, Barbara Kinney, Ralph Alswang, David Scull, and William Vasta—are an unusually talented group. They document every public event that Bill and I are part of, as well as some family events, whether they are in the house or halfway around the world. This is both heartening and terrifying. It means that moments are constantly being captured for history, but so too is every hairstyle, no matter how it looks!

We also have Press Office staff members who are available around the clock to handle inquiries from journalists, escort reporters and camera people, and provide background information for important announcements and events.

Policy experts grapple with hundreds of international and domestic issues each week, helping the President make decisions that affect the lives of millions of people across America and around the world. Members of the speechwriting and

Windor Building, and several town houses on Jackson Place. It is the collaboration among all of these staff members that makes every tour, dinner, White House conference, holiday reception, and policy announcement possible.

It is, for example, the men and women of the U.S. Secret Service who you first see when you come to the White House. They risk their lives to protect the President, his family, and every employee and visitor of the complex.

Bill and I are followed everywhere we go not only by the Secret Service, but usually scheduling staffs work closely with the President and me to develop events and remarks that most effectively convey the administration's vision here and abroad. Inevitably, as these views become public, there is a flood of phone calls that must be handled by the White House operators, and e-mails and letters that must be delivered by the mail carriers and opened and sorted by the hundreds of volunteers in the Office of Correspondence and answered by White House staff.

These staff and volunteers have come from all over the country. Their faces do not often appear in photographs, nor are their names likely to turn up in the news. Most work tirelessly behind the scenes. But their diligence, grace, and professionalism are evident every time a guest— be it a justice of the Supreme Court, a member of a championship team, a foreign head of state, or a family visiting their nation's capital for the first time— walks through the gate.

Right: White House photogapher Ralph Alswang and members of the press cover the 200th anniversary of the Marine Band, July 10, 1998.

"The President and Mrs. Clinton

REQUEST THE PLEASURE

OF THE COMPANY OF..."

Right: SSgt Regino Madrid, a member of the Marine Band, plays for guests at a State Dinner for President Vaclav Havel of the Czech Republic, September 16, 1998.

WELCOMING THE WORLD

I do not know if I have ever seen a larger or more spirited crowd on the South Lawn than the one that gathered to welcome Nelson Mandela for his first State Visit on October 4, 1994. Children waved South African and American flags; veteran politicians who had fought against apartheid brought their grandchildren to catch a glimpse of South Africa's first black president. Americans of all races and ethnicities crowded together to witness the arrival ceremony honoring a man whose courageous rise from prisoner to President had touched the hearts of people everywhere.

Occasions like the Mandela visit underscore the symbolic and strategic importance of welcoming world leaders to the White House. Each visit is a statement about America and her place in the world. Every element of the visit, from the meetings to the meals, is designed to strengthen the bonds of friendship with the visiting leader and highlight our two countries' shared aspirations for the future.

Entertaining in support of these goals is no simple task. I have tried to use these high-profile occasions to introduce the world's leaders to our very best thinkers, artists, and cuisine, and express American traditions in ways that honor the cultures of our visiting dignitaries. In doing so, we have one big advantage: the White House itself. The secret of its character is not only in the 18th-century chandeliers or priceless art, but in the history that comes to life every time Americans gather there.

In America's early days, Presidents did not travel beyond our borders and had little personal contact with people off our shores. President Jefferson was an exception. A former minister to Paris,

Right: Greeting President and Mrs. Clinton, President Mandela and his daughter Zinzi at the South Africa State Dinner, October 4, 1994 (from left to right): Alma Brown, Ron Brown, the first African-American to serve as Commerce Secretary, and Hazel O'Leary, the first African-American woman to serve as Secretary of Energy.

as President he even once received two diplomatic delegations on the very same day in 1805, one of Osage Indians, the other of Tunisian ministers. I would love to have a picture of that visit: the Tunisian minister in fine silk, velvet, and cashmere, studded with gold and pearls, crossing paths with the Indian leaders wearing deerskin and traditional body paint.

As our country has increasingly looked beyond our shores, the way we welcome the world at the White House has changed as well. In our time here, Bill and I have

Above: President Clinton takes President Mandela on a tour through the Lincoln Bedroom in 1994. The bronze sculpture on the tabletop is of Abraham Lincoln by Jeno Juszko. The frame in front of the sculpture contains a label describing the Lincoln history of the room. Right: President and Mrs. Clinton honor President Mandela at the South Africa State Dinner.

Above: President Clinton
greets President Andres
Pastrana of Colombia at
the White House on
October 28, 1998.

hosted leaders representing countries from every corner of the globe. These leaders are from emerging democracies, such as South Africa and the Czech Republic; old allies, such as the United Kingdom and France; former foes, such as Russia; neighbors, such as Mexico and Canada; and partners for peace, such as Israel, Jordan, and Egypt. In 1997 and 1998 we welcomed leaders from China to the White House, thereby symbolizing a new chapter in our relationship. I will never forget Premier Zhu Ronji of China recalling in his toast that he had memorized the Gettysburg Address as a schoolboy. He recited a section from memory, including the phrase "of the people, by the people, for the people"—a hope we hold for the Chinese people.

With every State Visit we are reminded of the depths of our alliances and the core values, such as freedom and democracy, that are our most valuable exports. In honoring President Jacques Chirac of France, the President noted that half of George Washington's troops at the decisive battle in Yorktown were French. "It is not an exaggeration," he said, "to say that the American people owe our liberty to France." Chirac responded by recalling his first encounter with Americans—U.S. GIs landing in Provence.

Because of the recent spread of democracy around the world, some of the

leaders we welcome were once in prison or exile. One of the most moving accounts of a leader who was touched by America came from President Fernando Henrique Cardoso of Brazil. In his toast, Cardoso recalled his time as an opposition leader when rumors of his imminent imprisonment drove him and his wife into hiding. "The very first visit I received was that of the American consul in São Paulo," he said. "He came to offer us a visa to the United States, where we could live in freedom."

Foreign leaders come to the house for three different types of visits, each of which demands different preparation. State Visits are reserved only for the designated head of state, who is often the king, queen, or president. Official Visits welcome the prime minister or other head of government. Working Visits include meetings with the President and Cabinet, but unlike Official and State Visits, they do not include arrival ceremonies or State Dinners.

Left: The President escorts Prime Minister Romano Prodi of Italy into the Diplomatic Reception Room.

At the beginning of each year, National Security Advisor Sandy Berger confers with the State Department and makes a proposal to the President, who ultimately decides which leaders receive an invitation to the White House. But plans can change as new opportunities arise. When Prime Minister Ehud Barak of Israel and his wife, Nava, visited soon after his election in June 1999, we initially planned an Official Working Visit with lunch for 18 people. But the excitement for their visit was so overwhelming that, with only five days to go, we turned it into a dinner for 500.

We did not know Ehud and Nava Barak yet, so, in addition to the formal events, we invited them to Camp David. The two men ended up talking into the wee hours of the morning. My husband had finally found another world leader who could stay up as late as he can. (This, of course, is a very critical skill during peace negotiations.)

While Mrs. Barak and I did not stay awake as late as our husbands did, we started a conversation on that trip about the violence plaguing young people's lives in both our countries. It was this conversation—and a shared

commitment—that spurred my visit to Tel Aviv in November 1999 for Mrs. Barak's conference on youth violence.

The importance of these types of social occasions should not be underestimated. Partnerships are built in different ways, and strong personal bonds between leaders allow both parties to speak frankly, building trust and friendships between individuals and countries.

During these foreign visits, I usually have coffee with the leader's spouse, many of whom I've met before in my travels. Sometimes we also organize or become involved in a public event to draw

Below: Mrs. Clinton exchanges gifts with Sheikh Hasina Wajed, Prime Minister of Bangladesh, February 3, 1997.

Above: Children with Korean and
American flags wait to greet President
and Mrs. Kim of Korea at the State
Arrival Ceremony, June 9, 1998.

attention to an issue about which we both care. For example, Cherie Booth, the wife of Prime Minister Tony Blair of the United Kingdom, is, like me, a lawyer and mother committed to improving the lives of children. When she visited a few years ago, we joined forces to raise awareness about the increasing number of children being abducted across international borders.

Above: MG Robert Foley and two Korean officers at the reception in the Blue Room after the State Arrival Ceremony. Left: President Clinton shows family pictures to President and Mrs. Kim during a tour of the Treaty Room.

DINNER
Honoring His Excellency
The President of the Republic of Korea
and Mrs. Kim Dae-jung

Hood River Spotted Prawn
Sweet Potato and Vidalia Onion Terrine
Marinated Tomato Salad
Chive Dressing

Honey Ginger Glazed Lamb
Crispy Rice Cake
Baby Bok Choy and Spring Vegetables

Mache Greens, Spinach and Young Lettuces
Baked Goat's Cheese and Grilled Portobello
25 Year Old Sherry Dressing

Mt. Soraksan Peaches and Fresh Raspberries
Peach Brandy Sabayon
Candied Ginger and Glazed Orange Rind

SHAFER *Chardonnay "Red Shoulder" 1996*
REX HILL *Pinot Noir Reserve 1994*
ROEDERER *L'ERMITAGE White House Cuvée 1991*

The White House
Tuesday, June 9, 1998

*Above: Pastry Chef
Mesnier and Assistant
Pastry Chef Franette
McCullough prepare a
dessert to be served in
chocolate boxes at the
Korean State Dinner.
Right: The President and
Mrs. Clinton, President
and Mrs. Kim pose for
photographers before
a State Dinner.*

Above: The dinner menu

*Opposite page: Mrs.
Clinton engages
guests in dinner
conversation.*

Left: Lyric soprano Hei-Kyung Hong, the evening's entertainment, chose a program of classical European and Korean composers to honor President and Mrs. Kim.

Above: Guests enjoying after-dinner dancing in the Grand Foyer.
Left: Vernon and Ann Jordan

Preparation for these visits begins months in advance, as the Office of Protocol starts a conversation with the visiting country about every detail of the trip. Some issues are obvious, such as the size of the delegation, the need for interpreters, and the musical and culinary tastes of the foreign leaders. But there is far more to negotiate if we want to make sure that we don't inadvertently offend our guests. Before we decide what colors or flowers to use, it's important to know, for example, that in China white is the color of mourning and in Japan chrysanthemums are the flower of death. When we're discussing the toasts at the State Dinner, it's important to know if our guests are prohibited from drinking alcohol or even from having it consumed in their presence, as is the case in some Muslim countries. We also negotiate the attire for the State Dinner, knowing that in some countries, such as Korea, the women come in national dress. Often, our visitors will want to know what color I'm wearing so that the other spouse and I don't clash. Another issue that can arise is the width and height of the podium, to make sure that shorter visiting leaders aren't overshadowed by a large podium or a tall American President.

Above: President and Mrs. Clinton
bid farewell to their guests beneath
the North Portico.

All of these decisions, large and small, are designed to make our guests feel as welcome and comfortable as possible. And that comfort includes their lodging. Our visitors usually stay on the other side of Pennsylvania Avenue at Blair House, where they can hold meetings and just plain rest and relax during an otherwise hectic visit. That hasn't always been the case. Blair House used to be a private home, and all visiting foreign leaders stayed at the White House until one night during Franklin Roosevelt's administration.

Mrs. Roosevelt was getting ready for bed when she suddenly noticed the presence of a large man who was not her husband. She wasn't sure whether to scream or attack him until he emerged from the shadows. It was Winston Churchill, who explained that he was looking for the President's bedroom because he wanted to continue a conversation they had started earlier. Mrs. Roosevelt gently, but firmly, sent him back to his room. It wasn't long after that she suggested that the government acquire an official guest house to help lodge foreign visitors.

Since then, a parade of great leaders have met there, slept there, and even made his-tory there—including President Truman, who lived there while the White House was renovated. For the foreign leaders who stay at the Blair House today, the general manager, Benedicte Valentiner, an employee of the State Department, tries to make it feel like home.

Although most of our guests arrive at Blair House the night before the visit, we welcome them formally in the morning. The arrival ceremony is usually held on the South Lawn, with the White House behind us and the Washington Monument off in the distance. When the foreign leader walks with the President down the red carpet to the stage, we hear hundreds of people, young and old, who trace their roots to the visiting leader's country cheering in their native tongue. We see members of the press, embassy staff, and our welcoming committee, which is a delegation of senior White House staff, administration officials, and Members of the Official Foreign Delegation. And lined up in front of us are the military men and women who represent all of our armed forces.

The ceremony is steeped in tradition. When the President walks down the grounds to review our troops with the accompanying leader, it is a gesture designed to showcase our military might. When we honor a head of state with a 21-gun salute (19 for a head of government), we recall the early days of our country when ships carrying foreign heads of state were greeted with the same ceremonial volley.

At every ceremony, a military band plays the national anthem of both countries, and the two leaders give welcoming remarks before entering the White House grounds to the music of trumpets sounding from the South Portico. And at every ceremony, the Old Guard Fife and Drum Corps, in colonial uniform, plays selections from the Revolutionary War period that pay tribute to our history of independence, including *Yankee Doodle Dandy,* which is always played—except when guests from the United Kingdom visit!

While the President and I try to reciprocate the warm welcomes we have received around the world, we have not matched the more than 500,000 people who greeted us in 1998 with music and

Below: President Jerry Rawlings and President Clinton proceed into the State Dinner, February 24, 1999.

dancing in Ghana, even though the temperature was well over 100 degrees. The weather posed a different challenge when we, in turn, welcomed President Jerry Rawlings of Ghana, a former fighter pilot who led his country to democracy, and his wife. That February day, temperatures dipped below freezing and President Rawlings had to buy an overcoat to protect him from the morning chill. We only hoped the warmth of our welcome overwhelmed the cold weather!

It is customary after the arrival ceremony for us to display the gifts that our guests have given us, gifts that express the visitors' unique heritage and the friendship between our nations. The First Lady of Israel Leah Rabin bought me a dove pin, a powerful symbol of her husband's continuing legacy of peace. When the President went to Japan in November 1998, Prime Minster Keizo Obuchi gave him two bonsai plants, which we sent to the National Arboretum, where they have stayed ever since—except for a few days in May 1999. When Prime Minister and Mrs. Obuchi visited us that month, we brought the plants to the White House and showcased

Below: Guests participate in the entertainment with contemporary jazz saxophonist Najee at the Ghana State Dinner.

Above: Mrs. Clinton and Nana Konadu Agyeman Rawlings, the First Lady of Ghana, after the Ghana State Arrival Ceremony.

them in the Blue Room in honor of the Obuchis. And we gave the Prime Minister a 300-year-old bonsai that had been grown in California.

When King Juan Carlos and Queen Sofia of Spain visited us in May 2000, I gave the Queen a handblown glass piece by Dale Chihuly and arranged for the artist to present it, knowing that the Queen admired his work. One of the most unique gifts that Bill gave a visitor was the one he gave Nelson Mandela. He knew President Mandela loved boxing, that he'd boxed as a child, and that, while in prison, he had heard a replay of Joe Lewis's historic 1938 rematch against Max Schmeling on the radio. So Bill asked every living heavyweight champion to write President Mandela a letter, and he put them together in a photo album, which included on its last page an unused ticket to Yankee Stadium for the Lewis-Schmeling fight.

Left: The traditional exchange of gifts. Mrs. Clinton presents Queen Sofia with the handblown glass Scarlet Basket *by Dale Chihuly as the artist looks on. The President presents King Juan Carlos with the traditional head of state gift, a handcrafted sterling silver cache pot from Tiffany & Co. with an engraved inscription to His Majesty, February 23, 1999.*

Above: The President and Mrs. Clinton and King Juan Carlos and Queen Sofia of Spain on the North Portico before the State Dinner.

Right: The United States welcoming committee, including the Diplomatic Corps, and the Spanish delegation view the State Arrival Ceremony for King Juan Carlos of Spain.

An invitation to a State Dinner is one of the most coveted invitations in America. Mrs. Kennedy increased the traditional guest list from 90 to 130. Although we now host as many as 400, narrowing down the final list is still a painstaking process. Many months in advance, we send out a request for suggestions throughout the State Department and White House, and the Social Office compiles all of these lists into one grid, paying attention to factors such as whether a potential guest has attended a previous dinner.

The President and I then make our selections, ensuring that the final list celebrates a diversity of prominent citizens—scholars, activists, artists, poets, business leaders, entertainers, members of Congress, and members of the press. Some people are always invited, such as Vice President and Mrs. Gore, Secretary of State Madeleine Albright, and high-ranking members of the visiting delegation. Others reflect the personal histories and relationships of our guests.

Right: A calligrapher's desk holds a stack of completed place cards.

On the occasion of the visit of
The Right Honorable
Tony Blair, M.P.
Prime Minister of the United Kingdom of
Great Britain and Northern Ireland
and Mrs. Blair

The President and Mrs. Clinton
request the pleasure of the company of

at a dinner to be held at
The White House
on Thursday, February 5, 1998
at seven-thirty o'clock

Black Tie

Left: An invitation to the Official Dinner for the Prime Minister of the United Kingdom, Tony Blair.

Above: The Social Office staff reviews protocol arrangements in the Grand Foyer for the February 5, 1998, Official Dinner in honor of Prime Minister Blair of the United Kingdom.

The guest list for the Ghana State Dinner, for example, included prominent African-Americans such as Pulitzer prize–winning writer Maya Angelou; baseball legend Hank Aaron; actress Angela Bassett; Washington, D.C., Mayor Anthony Williams; civil rights leader Jesse Jackson; Congressman John Lewis; track star Carl Lewis; soprano Denyce Graves; and Minnesota Vikings head coach Dennis Green. Bill and I were also pleased to have with us that evening Thomas Livingston, who in 1961 went to Ghana to teach English as the very first Peace Corps volunteer.

The dress code for State Dinners is usually black tie—with white tie reserved for kings and emperors. A handful of people always call to ask if white tie means top hats and canes for men, which it can, or long gowns for women, which it does. And there are always some last-minute fashion emergencies that can be solved using the stash of hosiery, shoes, dresses, and hair dryers that the Social Office keeps on hand.

In the weeks leading up to the big event, I work with the staff to create the right mood for the evening. When our guests walk into the State Dining Room, usually they see round tables covered with colorful cloths, White House china, and centerpieces of not only seasonal flowers but sometimes candles, grapes, artichokes, and other seasonal fruits and vegetables. And when guests sit down, they find menus (with the presidential seal) listing all the courses and wines. Over the years, I have seen people pass their menus around the table for their tablemates' signatures so they can take home a unique memento of the evening.

White House dinners have come a long way from the heart-stopping 29-course meals of the Grant administration. Mrs. Kennedy pared the meal down to four courses—and that number has stood the test of time. We have tried to serve food that is distinctly American, but that also

incorporates elements that pay tribute to our guests.

For the dinner honoring Premier Jiang Zemin of China, White House chefs spent three days fusing Asian and American cuisine into a Pacific Rim surf-and-turf. We started with lobster poached in lime leaves and lemongrass. Then we feasted on pepper-crusted Oregon beef from Asian cattle bred with American angus. The grand finale? Marzipan panda bears, mandarin tea tartlets, and orange sherbet swirled in giant chocolate oranges.

Dinner

On the occasion of the visit of
The Right Honorable
The Prime Minister of the United Kingdom
& Great Britain and Northern Ireland
and Mrs. Blair

Honey Mango Glazed Chicken
Spicy Vegetable "Noodles"
Herb Tuile

Grilled Salmon Fillet "Mignon"
Seared Portobello Mushroom
Tomato Shallot Fondue
Baby Vegetables and Balsamic Reduction

Marinated Fresh Mozzarella
Roasted Artichokes and Basil Tomatoes
Salad of Mache and Arugula
Lemon Oregano Dressing

"Strawberries and Cream"
Devonshire Sauce
Brandy Snaps   Shortbread
Honey Nougat   Chocolate Fudge

NEWTON *Chardonnay* "Unfiltered" 1995
SWANSON *Sangiovese* 1995
MUMM *Napa Valley* DVX 1993

The White House
Thursday, February 5, 1998

Left: The dinner menu
Below: In the kitchen, Mrs. Clinton checks on preparations for the United Kingdom Official Dinner (from left to right): part-time chefs Paula Moutsos, Jason Stitt, and Francis O'Dear.

Above: President and Mrs. Clinton, and Prime Minister and Mrs. Blair in the Blue Room after the morning's official Arrival Ceremony in 1998.

Right: Mrs. Clinton, Elton John, Stevie Wonder, Jeffrey Katzenberg, and Vice President Gore at the afternoon rehearsal for the United Kingdom Official Dinner.

Some of the most successful diplomacy happens not at the negotiating table but after dinner, during the evening's featured entertainment. Nothing can knock down barriers of language and culture better than experiencing a beautiful aria or concerto. And no one knocked down more barriers than President Boris Yeltsin of Russia. After dinner, Yeltsin, captivated by the Yale Russian Chorus's rendition of a traditional Russian song, rushed forward and wrapped the conductor in a bear hug, planting a kiss on each cheek. The conductor was deeply touched—

that is, once he recovered from his shock. Yeltsin had approached from behind, and the only warning the conductor had was the widening eyes of his singers!

We also try to tailor the entertainment to our guests. For President Carlos Saul Menem of Argentina, we tangoed with actor Robert Duvall and Luciana Pedrazza. For Prime Minister Blair, we arranged a transatlantic performance by Elton John and Stevie Wonder; their rendition of *That's What Friends Are For* summed up our nations' close relations.

Above left: Mrs. Clinton and Mrs. Gore in the Yellow Oval Room, awaiting dinner guests.

Above right: The President and Mrs. Clinton, and Prime Minister and Mrs. Blair share a private moment in the Yellow Oval Room before the State Dinner.

Left: The Presidential Color Team escorts the Clintons and the Blairs down the Grand Staircase to join their guests below.

Above left: In the receiving
line, Barbara Walters and
Senator John Warner greet
President and Mrs. Clinton
and Prime Minister and
Mrs. Blair at the Official
Dinner.
Above right: Seated for the
entertainment, two dearly
missed friends: John F.
Kennedy Jr. and Carolyn
Bessette Kennedy.

The artists, who are really ambassadors-for-an-evening, carefully choose their music to please the guest of honor. When cellist Mstislav Rostropovich, former music director of the National Symphony Orchestra, performed for Emperor Akihito of Japan, his choice of the scherzo from the *Sonata for Cello and Piano* by Shostakovich had multiple meanings. Emperor Akihito plays the cello and his wife plays the piano. Also, when Akihito's father, Emperor Hirohito, visited the White House in 1975, the entertainment was piano. So the cello and piano duet united the father's and the son's visits.

The names that have played at State and Official Dinners are a virtual who's who of the greatest musical performances of our time—from Kathleen Battle to Judy Collins, from Yo-Yo Ma to the Modern Jazz Quartet. Yet even the most seasoned performers have confessed to us that they get nervous playing at the White House. Many have said that their White House performances are the highlight of their careers. At the Moroccan State Dinner in June 2000, Philip Bailey of Earth, Wind, and Fire moved us all when he exclaimed, "Back in the fourth grade when I started beating on trash cans with chicken feet poles and mimicking Elvis Presley, I would have never dreamed that I would be standing here. . . ."

Of course sometimes it is an amateur who steals the show. Twelve-year-old Cory

Pesaturo first met the President after playing his accordion during a White House Christmas reception. When Cory was having his picture taken, the President asked him to play and was so delighted by what he heard that he invited Cory back to perform at the Hungarian State Dinner. During dessert, we always hear from the Strolling Strings, small musical groups from either the Marine Band, the Army Band, or the Air Force Band, which move through the room playing selections to honor the visiting leader. But when the Marine Strolling Strings walked in this time, Cory was right next to its director, Charles Corrado. As Cory launched into the popular song *Beer Barrel Polka,* the crowd rose to its feet, and President Arpad Goncz of Hungary went to Cory's side to offer praise for his playing.

Top right: Twelve-year-old Cory Pesaturo delights guests at the Hungary State Dinner, June 9, 1999. Right: The President and First Lady congratulate soprano Kathleen Battle and her accompanist Joseph Jaubert at the State Dinner for President Boris Yeltsin of Russia, September 27, 1994.

Above: Mrs. Clinton and the Empress of Japan greet the U.S. and Japanese delegations after the State Arrival Ceremony for Emperor Akihito of Japan, June 13, 1994.

Far left: The President and the Emperor of Japan in the Diplomatic Reception Room after the ceremony.
Left: The First Lady and the Empress of Japan in the Entrance Hall.

Right: Mstislav Rostropovich performed at the 1994 Japan State Dinner.
Far right: The President and First Lady, and the Emperor and Empress of Japan in the Second Floor Corridor. Two musicians from the Marine Band are witnesses to history.

Below: Mrs. Clinton, the Emperor of Japan, President Clinton, the Empress, and Vice President Gore at the State Dinner head table.

These events are about much more than fun. United States foreign policy is strengthened every time the White House welcomes the world, whether it's the peace treaty signed in the Rose Garden between President Fujimori of Peru and President Mahuad of Ecuador in October 1998 or the promise Prime Minister Sharif of Pakistan made not to escalate war in Kashmir after his meeting with the President on the Fourth of July, 1999.

Bill and I are very fortunate that our time in the White House has given us more occasions to celebrate peace than contemplate war. For example, we welcomed a democratically elected president from Nigeria and brought all the leaders involved in the Northern Ireland peace process, including those of Sein Fein, to the White House. For the first time, the world saw the Prime Minister of Israel, Yitzhak Rabin, and Palestinian leader Yasser Arafat shake hands.

In 1994 Bill and I had the privilege of hosting a dinner that would have been unthinkable just a few years before. We honored King Hussein of Jordan and Yitzhak Rabin one year after the Mideast peace pact was signed on the White House lawn. Rabin and Hussein were seasoned warriors and, for many years, avowed enemies. Yet they found a way to put aside ancient hatreds, lay down their arms, and fight for peace instead.

On that magical evening, King Hussein recalled his four decades of visits to the White House and the progress that allowed such seemingly disparate leaders finally to break bread together. "I dreamed about it," he said. "I prayed for it." Both men are gone now, one lost to cancer, the other to an assassin's bullet. But I do know that the spirit of their last and greatest pursuit—peace—lives on in this house and in the hearts of those who come here in its name.

Below: Before the signing of the September 13, 1993, Middle East peace agreement.

Above: On October 1, 1996, the President hosted a working lunch in the Library with Chairman Yasser Arafat of the Palestinian Authority, Prime Minister Benjamin Netanyahu of Israel, and King Hussein of Jordan. The Middle East Peace talks at Wye Plantation took place that week.

Right: President Clinton presides over a historic handshake: Israeli Prime Minister Yitzhak Rabin, and Palestinian leader Yasser Arafat, September 21, 1993.

Above: August 8, 1998, the President and Mrs. Clinton, and King Hussein and Queen Noor of Jordan enjoyed a quiet dinner together on the Truman Balcony during one of the last times the King visited the White House. Right: A view from the podium at the July 25, 1994, signing of the peace declaration between Israel and Jordan.

At no time was that sentiment more true than on April 24, 1999, during the celebration of the 50th anniversary of the North Atlantic Treaty Organization and its role in building a more peaceful and democratic world. The NATO Summit was, without question, the biggest challenge I faced as hostess. We brought together leaders from 44 countries for the largest gathering of foreign heads of state ever to assemble at the White House.

To most people, this sounds like an opportunity for a memorable event. But if you are a member of the Social Office or the Office of Protocol, the logistics alone are enough to make your hair stand on end. Forty-four world leaders meant 44 motorcades that needed to move in and out of the White House at the same time, 44 embassies in need of assistance, 44 security details, 44 press corps, and 44 official delegations (each ranging in size from 50 to 300 people, many of whom needed their own translators). It also meant working with the D.C. government to close down some local streets for the day.

It seemed that things were just beginning to get under control when the NATO alliance decided to intervene in Kosovo. Overnight, the tone of the event had to change from celebratory to subdued.

Because of the conflict, we also knew that leaders would need to work while they were here, so we set up meeting rooms and telephone lines in the Map Room, the China Room, and the Vermeil Room.

It was more important than ever that the first night's dinner express a sense of unity. With that in mind, I remembered something from the trip the President and I had made to Santiago, Chile, for the Summit of the Americas. There are many beautiful things to admire in Chile, but on that visit I was captivated by, of all things, a table. It was in the shape of a crescent. It seated every leader and spouse. Everyone could see each other. Everyone was united. Everyone was equal.

That was exactly what I wanted for the heads of state and spouses of all 19 NATO countries, including the three new members: Hungary, Poland, and the Czech Republic. The entire weekend was, in some sense, a reunion for everyone. The President and I had met many of the leaders and their spouses in our travels, and we were eager to welcome them here and show them the house and its history. Friday's dinner was special from the moment we sat down and everyone realized that we were all at the same table (in more than one sense of the word) to Jessye Norman's finale. I

Above: Reflected in a mirror, Mrs. Clinton and Mrs. Daphne Simitis, wife of the Prime Minister of Greece, discuss the paintings in the Green Room, including the Georgia O'Keeffe (at left above the secretary), April 23, 1999. Mrs. Simitis is an admirer of O'Keeffe's work.

Above: A mirrored architectural backdrop creates the illusion of a grand room inside the pavilion on the South Lawn.

Above: Secretary General Javier Solano of NATO, President Clinton, and the First Lady at the head table at dinner on Saturday evening, April 24, 1999.

daughters of NATO's founders. It was clear that having 44 delegations arrive at one gate would create a bottleneck worse than any rush hour traffic, so we had guests arrive in rotation at three entrances: the North Portico, the East Portico, and the West Lobby.

Mother Nature was kind enough to give us a perfect April evening. For the look and feel of the entire night, I turned to my friend Robert Isabell, who designed the interior of the South Lawn pavilion to look like an extension of the White House and foster a sense of elegance and intimacy. From its architectural moldings to its stately columns and gilded mirrors, Isabell's creation gave everyone the illusion of being inside a great hall that had stood for centuries. It inspired international variations of "Wow!" all evening.

think most leaders had heard her beautiful voice at some point before, but when she burst into an a cappella rendition of *Amazing Grace,* she outdid herself.

While Friday's gathering was an intimate occasion in the East Room, Saturday's dinner involved more than 900 guests, including former and current heads of state from around the world, former U.S. secretaries of state, and the sons and

As the leaders entered this beautiful pavilion one by one, I made sure they stopped on a raised platform so they could be seen by everyone, including their own press corps. After dinner, American opera stars Thomas Hampson and Renée Fleming sang a medley of songs from many of the countries in their respective languages. The Czech delegation stood and cheered when they heard a favorite song in their own language. Many guests told us with

great emotion what it meant on that night to hear music in their native tongue.

In his remarks, the President captured the real meaning of the evening when he said, "In Kosovo, the peace is threatened by the oldest demon of society—the fear and hatred of the other. Tonight we remember that the burden of defending freedom and peace is lighter when it is shouldered by so many."

When we said good-bye on Sunday, we were exhausted and exhilarated, but NATO was stronger than ever, and so too was the world's determination to stop ethnic cleansing and end the war. The unified stance solidified that weekend was yet another reminder of the importance of NATO's alliance and the incredible power of the White House to welcome, and ultimately change, the world.

Above: The crescent-shaped table for the NATO anniversary dinner in the East Room on Friday evening, April 23, 1999.

$\mathscr{A}$T A MAJOR EVENT LIKE THE VISIT OF PRESIDENT HAVEL, EVERYTHING MUST FLOW SEAMLESSLY.

Right: Director of Logistics Laura Schwartz reviews pages of carefully scripted preparations to ensure every detail and contingency has been covered. Left: Members of the Military District of Washington ensure that position markers are placed properly.

Left: Houseman Bernard Ward vacuums the red carpet leading up the steps of the North Entrance before guests arrive for the 1998 State Dinner in honor of President Havel of the Czech Republic.
Opposite page: An invitation to the dinner

TICK-TOCK

MANY AMERICANS HAVE AN IMAGE OF A STATE Visit: the leaders reviewing the troops at the Arrival Ceremony or elegantly dressed guests moving through a receiving line. But few realize that leading up to these high-profile moments are months of work. Below is a count-down of one visit, that of President Václav Havel of the Czech Republic in September 1998. While the details may vary from country to country, the timeline is typical of our preparations for a State Visit from any foreign leader.

The President and Mrs. Clinton request the pleasure of the company of

at a dinner to be held at
The White House
on Wednesday, September 16, 1998
at seven-thirty o'clock

Black Tie

On the occasion of the visit of
His Excellency
Václav Havel
President of the Czech Republic
and Mrs. Havlová

SPRING

When the State Department and National Security Council proposed inviting the President of the Czech Republic for a State Visit, the President agreed wholeheartedly. The time was right to recognize Václav Havel for his accomplishments in advancing democracy and human rights in Central and Eastern Europe. The Czech Republic was about to join NATO, and there were issues that could best be addressed in a face-to-face visit. As soon as the Czechs accepted our invitation, planning for the visit began.

JULY

On July 17, the Press Office announced President Havel's acceptance of our invitation to visit from September 15 to 18. The Social Office and the United States Chief of Protocol began meeting with the Czech embassy to prepare for the visit and learn about the Havels' favorite music, flowers, and food so we could tailor the dinner to their tastes.

AUGUST

Compiling an invitation list is a time-consuming art, which begins with the solicitation of suggestions from White House staff by Deputy Social Secretaries Sharon Kennedy and Kim Widdess. In early August, Social Secretary Capricia Marshall brought the President and me binders containing lists of proposed guests and their affiliations to the visiting country. Once the President and I decided whom to invite, Rick Paulus, Rick Muffler, and Estelle Stolz in the Calligraphy Office

**THE STATE VISIT TO WASHINGTON D.C. OF
HIS EXCELLENCY VACLAV HAVEL PRESIDENT OF THE CZECH REPUBLIC
AND MRS. HAVLOVA**

STATE DINNER
WEDNESDAY, SEPTEMBER 16, 1998
STATE FLOOR
7:15 p.m.

Attire:	**Black Tie**
Guest Arrival:	**East Gate, 6:45 p.m.**
Principal Arrival:	**North Portico, 7:15 p.m. (Press)**
Private Reception:	**Yellow Oval Room, 7:20 p.m.**
Receiving Line:	**Grand Foyer/Cross Hall, 7:55 p.m. (Press)**
Dinner/Toasts:	**East Room, 8:35 p.m. (Press for remarks)**
Entertainment:	**East Room, 10:20 p.m. (Press for remarks)**
Departure:	**North Portico (Principals) East Gate (Guests) South Portico (Delegation)**

2:00 p.m.   Technical run-through for entertainment.

4:00 p.m.   Press preview.

5:30 p.m.   Social Aide walk-throughs w/SICs of each area.

6:30 p.m.   In place time for staff, Social Aides.

6:45 p.m.   Guests arrive to the East Portico. Guests check their coats at Family Theater and proceed to the Booksellers area where they are announced to press by a Social Aide.

SIC Arrivals: Bronson Frick
Guest Arrival inside: Tibbie Turner
SIC Press set-up: Sharon Kennedy Gill
SIC Ground Floor movements/escort cards/Delegation arrival: Kim Widdess
Refer to staffing chart for all other staffing.

State Dinner Scenario   1

GUEST ARRIVAL/GROUND FLOOR NOTES: Car Parkers; door openers; mags inside East Portico; coat check in Family Theater; sculpture garden lights on; press set up in Booksellers; WHCA stand-up mic in position for SA press announce (also used as carriage call for departures); escort cards and table outside China Room; wooden screens up on west side of Dip Room on Ground Floor; flute trio at East Landing; single violinist at stair bottom; coat rack in China Room for Delegation members arriving at the Diplomatic Reception Room; Color Guard hold in China Room/behind wooden screens on Ground Floor; small monitor outside Ladies Mezzanine for social reporters to hear bookseller announces.

Guests enter the First Ladies Hall to pick up escort cards at stair bottom and are escorted to the State Dining Room by Social Aides (will not hold for Color Guard, SA will begin escorts as guests arrive).

Guests are announced into the State Dining Room.
SIC State Floor: Laura Schwartz
2 Volunteers in SDR

STATE DINING ROOM RECEPTION NOTES: Violin in Grand Foyer playing as guests enter to greet the Social Secretary; Marine String Quartet w/piano in south west corner of SDR; Social Aides depart down Ushers steps back to Ground Floor after escort; 2 Volunteers in SDR; cocktails passed inside room - not to build up congestion at doorway; WHCA announce position in Cross Hall corner - entrance to the State Dining Room on North side.

7:00 p.m.   Open phone line established with Ushers Office, Residence, Carlos Elizondo.
347-0399 x575 or ask for Lincoln Room
(All cues coordinated by Military Aide and L. Schwartz)

The Vice President and Mrs. Gore, The Secretary of State and guest arrive to the South Portico (separately) and proceed to hold in the Red Room until arrival of principals.
Escort: 1 Social Aide

7:10 p.m.   **President Havel and Mrs. Havlova** ready to depart Blair House for the White House with Yellow Oval Room guests.

7:13 p.m.   The Color Guard proceeds up Grand Staircase to the Residence; guests held on Ground Floor while Principals and Yellow Oval Room guests arrive.
Note: Escorts up grand staircase stop for color guard movement cue from Laura Schwartz.

On these pages: Logistics schedules for the Havel State Dinner, used by the White House staff involved in the event. Other events of the State Visit required equally detailed memos. The President and First Lady, and Vice President and Mrs. Gore received versions tailored to their participation in the event.

Note: Color Guard will cue off L. Schwartz and the President's departure from Blair House.

7:13 p.m.   **THE PRESIDENT** and **MRS. CLINTON** depart living quarters via elevator and proceed to North Portico.

**Military Aide to confirm departure of President Havel and Mrs. Havlova from Blair House.*

*** SDR doors closed for principals' arrival; escorts to reception halted.*

**** VP, MEG and Albright + guest taken to Yellow Oval Room from Red Room.*

7:15 p.m.   President Havel and Mrs. Havlova arrive to the North Portico and are greeted by **THE PRESIDENT** and **MRS. CLINTON** at the top of the North Portico stairs.

THE FOUR PRINCIPALS pose for photo on the steps of the North Portico:

Official Photo:
(left to right)

**President Havel
THE PRESIDENT
Mrs. Havlova
MRS. CLINTON**
(Open Press)

Interpreter Note: Interpreter already on the State Floor and proceeds following the Official Photo up back stairs to the Yellow Oval Room for reception.

THE FOUR PRINCIPALS proceed to the Yellow Oval Room via elevator.

7:16 p.m.   Ambassador French proceeds to the North Portico to greet the Czech Republic Delegation Yellow Oval Room participants.

Ambassador French escorts the Czech Republic guests to the Yellow Oval Room via elevator or Grand Staircase.
Note: Ambassador French has escort cards for Czech Republic guests in the Yellow Oval Room.

State Dinner Scenario   3

Yellow Oval Room Guests

The United States
The President and Mrs. Clinton
The Vice President and Mrs. Gore
Secretary of State Albright and Katherine Silva
US Ambassador Jenonne Walker

The Czech Republic
President Havel and Mrs. Havlova
Foreign Minister Jan Kavan
Ambassador Alexandr Vondra and Mrs. Vondrova

Interpreters:
Mrs. Brabcova and Mr. Dusek
Mr. Borek and Mr. Reznicek

7:20 p.m.   Social Aides resume escorts into the State Dining Room.
(Escorts to resume as soon as North Portico arrivals are taken to Yellow Oval - take cue from Laura Schwartz)

7:25 p.m.   The Official Delegation of the Czech Republic departs Blair House to West Exec., and enters SW Gate en route to the Diplomatic Reception Room.
Contact: David Pryor
Contact Dip Room: Laura Wills /Kim Widdess

7:30 p.m.   Remaining members of the Official Delegation of the Czech Republic arrive to the Diplomatic Reception Room via South West Gate and are escorted by Social Aides to the State Dining Room for a reception.
Note: Coat rack in China Room for Delegation, members not attending dinner proceed to Map Room to hold; Protocol to have Delegation escort cards.
Contact: Laura Wills, David Pryor and Kim Widdess

7:40 p.m.   Social Secretary Marshall and Ambassador French escort Yellow Oval Room guests (**save PRINCIPALS**) via elevator to the State Dining Room, where they are announced by a Social Aide.
Note: Social Aide in place at elevator to greet and line up Yellow Oval Guests as they are announced into reception.

***Receiving line note:** Pre-positioning of table hosts in Red Room begins.*
Contact: Kim Widdess/Social Aide OIC of Receiving Line

7:45 p.m.   The Color Guard proceeds to the Yellow Oval Room. The Officer In Charge requests permission from **THE PRESIDENT** to secure the Colors. The Color Guard secures the Colors and proceeds out of the Yellow Oval Room down the Grand Staircase.
Contact: Gary Walters

State Dinner Scenario   4

7:50 p.m.   **THE FOUR PRINCIPALS** are announced to HONORS and proceed down the <u>Grand Staircase</u>. **THE FOUR PRINCIPALS** pause <u>at base of stairs</u> for Official Photo.

OFFICIAL PHOTO:
(left to right)
President Havel
THE PRESIDENT
Mrs. Havlova
MRS. CLINTON

President Havel is to the right, the position of honor, of **THE PRESIDENT.

PRINCIPAL NOTE: Following the photo, **The Four Principals** and the press HOLD while the Color Guard reposition in Cross Hall. The Military Aide escorts **The Four Principals** into the Blue Room to hold for 3-4 minutes for press to reposition for receiving line.

> **BLUE ROOM NOTE**: North door of Blue Room closed to Red Room, screen in south doorway of Blue Room and Red Room.

CROSS HALL REPOSITIONING NOTES: While the four principals hold in Blue Room, SDR doors are closed; guests are already lined through the Red Room for receiving line- and are now brought up to Social Secretary Position in the Cross Hall; press pool, cables, equipment, rope and stanchion are moved to Cross Hall side of Foyer.

Once press is in place, the Military Aide leads The Four Principals into the <u>Cross Hall</u> to line up for receiving line under the <u>Seal of the President</u>.

RECEIVING LINE ORDER
(flow west to east)

THE PRESIDENT
President Havel
MRS. CLINTON
Mrs. Havlova

Interpreter Note: Interpreter behind the Principals (like arrival receiving line)
Press Note: Expanded Pool press for receiving line.

RECEIVING LINE FORMAT: Receiving line flows west to east. Guests proceed to receiving line from <u>Red Room</u>. Announce mic between Red and Blue Room doors; guests are announced by a Social Aide as they proceed through receiving line. Guests are directed to the <u>East Room</u> where they are seated for dinner.

NOTE: The Official Delegation of the Czech Republic and the American Delegation are the last to proceed through the receiving line. The table hosts are the first to proceed through the line.

8:35 p.m.   Upon conclusion of the receiving line, **THE FOUR PRINCIPALS** proceed to the <u>Blue Room</u> for a brief hold.

         THE FOUR PRINCIPALS are announced into the <u>East Room</u> to a musical fanfare and proceed to their tables <u>via Cross Hall.</u>

PRESS COVERAGE OF TOASTS; ENTRY AND EXIT:
ENTRY
Press staff: Julianne Corbet, Mike Teague, J. Mason, Sharon Kennedy Gill
On the Four Principals' entry to the East Room, a riser and stanchion will be brought into Cross Hall doorway into the East Room. Two press office staff will precede press and walk in with the residence staff in charge of placing stanchion to control cameras and to keep a reasonable distance from guests. At the same time a third press office staffer will bring the pencils into the north doorway to the East Room, also preceding press to keep a reasonable distance from guests. 2 lights on stix (already pre-set in the afternoon) are turned on.

EXIT
Following toasts press are taken back to the briefing room via the North Portico.

Interpreters Note: Interpreters pre-positioned in East Room.
Contact: Chris Major

8:45 p.m.   Once all guests are seated and the press is repositioned, **THE PRESIDENT** proceeds to the <u>Eagle Lectern</u>.

Toast by **THE PRESIDENT**.

Response by **President Havel**.

Interpreter Note: Consecutive interpretation from WHCA toast lectern w/piano lamp at south west corner of room.

8:55 p.m.   Following toasts, dinner is served.

Entertainment Note: String quartet repositions to Cross Hall doorway to East Room to play during dinner.

DURING DINNER NOTES: All Social Aides and staff/volunteers eat in Mess WITH TICKET or remain on Ground Floor, Ground Floor will be kept alert of course and dinner movements, no one should be on State Floor or in Usher's Office; East Room doors will be open during dinner, Cross Hall MUST remain clear at all times; Marine Serenade Dance Band set up in Grand Foyer at this time for dancing.

9:30 p.m.   After dinner guests (4) arrive <u>East Appointments Gate</u> and proceed to hold in <u>Diplomatic Reception Room</u> until cue from Laura Schwartz.
Contact: Bronson Frick, one Social Aide positioned in Diplomatic Reception Room.

9:50 p.m.   Strolling Strings to play three songs after dessert is placed on tables. Following the strings, a flute or other musicians stay to play in Cross Hall entrance to the East Room during transition to entertainment. Wait for cue from Laura.

TRANSITION TO ENTERTAINMENT
Tables cleared, coffee served, programs placed on tables.

         Press arrive North Door and Cross Hall doorway to East Room and proceed to riser.
         SIC: Sharon Kennedy Gill

10:15/20 p.m.   Off-stage announce of entertainment.
         Note: Announce from Green Room.

         Performance begins.

10:45 p.m.   Performance concludes.

         THE PRESIDENT proceeds to stage to thank performers.

         WHCA Note: Wired microphone in place behind gold curtain if needed for after entertainment remarks.
         *Note: President Havel may wish to join **THE PRESIDENT** in remarks.*

         THE PRESIDENT makes brief remarks.

         President Havel has the option to make brief remarks.

         *Interpretation Note: Consecutive Interpretation if **President Havel** speaks*

---

         in Czech at podium, same location in SW corner.

         Press Note: Expanded Pool for entertainment

10:50 p.m.   Military Aide escorts **THE PRESIDENT, MRS. CLINTON, President Havel and Mrs. Havlova** to the <u>North Portico</u>.

10:55 p.m.   **THE PRESIDENT** and **MRS. CLINTON** bid farewell to **President Havel and Mrs. Havlova**.

         Note: Members of The Official Delegation of The Czech Republic depart White House from the <u>Diplomatic Reception Room</u> en route to <u>Blair House</u> following the departure of the **President Havel and Mrs. Havlova**.
         Contact: Protocol

11:00 p.m.   **THE PRESIDENT** and **MRS. CLINTON** proceed to the <u>Grand Foyer</u> for the first dance.

         Guests proceed to the <u>Grand Foyer</u> for dancing.

GRAND FOYER - DANCING NOTES: liquors in Parlor Rooms - set during entertainment; Marine Serenade Dance Band in place.

TBD   **THE PRESIDENT** and **MRS. CLINTON** depart the <u>Grand Foyer</u> and return to the <u>Private Residence</u>.

         Guests depart <u>East Portico</u>.
         SIC Departures: Bronson Frick

Top: The President and Mrs. Clinton greet President Havel and Mrs. Havlová. Middle: Commander of the Troops COL Gregory Gardner leads the two Presidents as they review the troops. Bottom: Entering the White House at the completion of the ceremony.

began lettering the invitations. After hours of proofing, stuffing, sealing, and stamping by Social Office assistant Tibbie Turner, the invitations were mailed.

EARLY SEPTEMBER

There is no job I enjoy more in the weeks leading up to a State Dinner than sampling the menu and working with the chefs until the dishes are just right. For the Czech visit, Executive Chef Walter Scheib developed a menu featuring a first course of pheasant consommé over ravioli with wild mushrooms, and a main course of roasted salmon with carrot and corn risotto. Pastry Chef Roland Mesnier planned an elaborate composition of caramel rum raisin ice cream, poached pears, and sour cherry pate.

To create the right mood for the event, Capricia, Nancy Clarke, and I brainstormed about tablecloths, table settings, flower arrangements, and china. We decided tables would be lit by gold candelabras from the vermeil collection, surrounded by beige and peach roses, white hydrangea, and votive candles. Since only two collections of china are large enough to serve a State Dinner, we often blend the sets. We decided that the Havel dinner would be served using Truman

Left: President Havel gives remarks at the State Arrival Ceremony. Right: Watching the ceremony are: Carolyn Shelton, GEN Henry Shelton, Chairman of the Joint Chiefs of Staff, and Secretary of State Madeleine Albright.

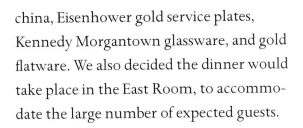

Above: The Old Guard Fife and Drum Corps

china, Eisenhower gold service plates, Kennedy Morgantown glassware, and gold flatware. We also decided the dinner would take place in the East Room, to accommodate the large number of expected guests.

And, of course, the entertainment that would cap the evening would have to be just right to send off our honored guests on a high note. In this case, the usually difficult choice of entertainment was an easy one. President Havel let us know that the music of Lou Reed had inspired him while he fought communism and consoled him during his time in prison. In fact, Lou Reed had once been part of a band called the Velvet Underground, and the struggle Havel had been part of was

called the Velvet Revolution. So we moved quickly to secure Lou Reed to entertain for the evening.

We also realized that the Havels would be in Washington the night we were planning to host a special "Millennium Evening" celebrating jazz. Knowing the role this uniquely American music played in inspiring democracy around the world, we decided to extend an invitation to the Havels to join us for this special event and were delighted when they accepted.

SEPTEMBER 15

No matter how far in advance we plan, the day before a formal arrival is always a busy

Below: Lou Reed's guitars await rehearsal in the Blue Room. Above the table is a portrait of President James Monroe by Samuel F. B. Morse.

one and this one was no different. To make the events flow smoothly, Director of Logistics Laura Schwartz conducted afternoon rehearsals with military aides, social aides, and the Color Guard. Director of Entertainment Debby McGinn coordinated sound-checks for the performers. Calligraphers lettered the place cards and escort envelopes, while Capricia spent hours finalizing seating assignments. Once the President and I approved the seating, Capricia alerted the calligraphers so they could begin placing assignments in each escort envelope. Letters were faxed to table hosts, who would know in advance those dining with them and would assist in guiding our guests through the evening.

Nancy and her staff set out the flowers and created bases for the table arrangements. The Usher's Office coordinated a final sprucing-up of the house—touching up the paint on the North Portico, hanging baskets with cascades of flowers between the columns on the State Floor, and placing lush greenery in the area where guest arrivals would be announced to the press.

Meanwhile, President Havel and Mrs. Havlová arrived at 5 p.m. at Andrews Air Force Base. Ambassador Mary Mel French and Czech Republic Ambassador to the United States Alexander Vondra welcomed them with a red carpet, military formations, and a motorcade escort to Blair House. There they rested up in preparation for the long day ahead of them.

SEPTEMBER 16

On the day of a State Visit, we welcome our guests formally at the morning Arrival Ceremony and host a formal dinner in the evening. But sandwiched between these moments is a day that never stops.

7:00 A.M.
After making a final assessment of the weather, Laura Wills and the Protocol staff, the Military District of Washington, and White House staff converged on the South Lawn to prepare for the Arrival Ceremony, ensuring everyone's place was clearly marked and the red carpet was immaculately extended to the South Drive.

8:00 A.M.
Guests invited for the Arrival Ceremony, including senior administration officials, citizens with Czech roots, our visitors' embassy staff, and children from area schools, began arriving at their designated gates and viewing areas, where they

"Lou Reed, one of the fathers of the American Underground, is a living legend. He, along with Andy Warhol and other one time co-creators of a new type of American self-realization, and consequently the unrepeatable atmosphere of the 'sixties, affected even the Czech lands with his works. During the 'sixties, hundreds of bands there were born and dissolved, inspired not only by the famed Beatles, Dylan, and Rolling Stones, but also by a group lesser known even in its homeland, the Velvet Underground.

Following the occupation by the nations of the Warsaw Pact thirty years ago, a renewed totalitarian system naturally began to damage these groups. Many of them disbanded, many, due to existing reasons, changed their style, repertoire, name and even their hair style. Some attempted to save what they could at the price of certain compromises, and only a microscopic part remained themselves without any kind of concession.

These few groups were persecuted in numerous ways for years, and not because they were a political opposition, but only because they acted free. The best known of these was a group called the Plastic People of the Universe, whose great inspiration was the Velvet Underground. The persecution of the Plastics culminated in 1976 with the imprisonment of its members and their friends. When this occurred, a sense of solidarity on a larger scale reemerged in the Czech lands. This sense ultimately led to the first widespread movement for human rights in the entire Soviet camp—Charter 77. It is therefore possible to say that the music of that group became a kind of guide or symbol for the struggle for freedom in the Czech lands.

I am very grateful that President Clinton honored my request to invite Lou Reed to this dinner. I am no less grateful that Lou Reed, one of the founders of the Velvet Underground, invited the long-time leader of the Plastic People of the Universe, Milan Hlavsa, to perform with him. Joining us on this historic night, are two legends from our two nations who both, in one way or another, are bound with the ideal of freedom."

His Excellency Václav Havel
President of the Czech Republic
September 16, 1998

SELECTIONS BY

Lou Reed
Vocals and Guitar

Michael Rathke
Guitar

Tony Smith
Drums

Fernando Saunders
Bass

Special Guest
Milan Hlavsa
Bass

Left: President Havel requested that Lou Reed perform at the State Dinner, and personally wrote a message for the program.

Left: At the afternoon rehearsal, President Havel surprises Lou Reed and his band.

DINNER
in honor of
His Excellency Václav Havel
President of the Czech Republic
and Mrs. Havlová

Gingered Pheasant Consommé
Ravioli of Chantrelles and Sweet Potatoes
Pheasant Confit on Lemon Spinach

Roasted Salmon with Honey Spice Glaze
Carrot and Corn Rissotto
Charred Tomato Compote

Baked Artichokes
Oregano Marinated Goat Cheese
Late Summer Greens and Chive
Garlic Dressing

Caramel Rum Raisin Ice Cream
Poached Pear in Red Wine Sauce
Sour Cherry Pate de Fruit
Hazelnut Gianduja   *Vanilla Pretzel*

Lewis "Reserve" Chardonnay 1996
Archery Summit Pinot Noir 1994
Roederer "White House Cuvée" 1991

THE WHITE HOUSE   WEDNESDAY, SEPTEMBER 16, 1998

Above: A butler prepares for the State Dinner under the watchful eye of George Washington.

Below: During a press preview prior to the State Dinner, Capricia Marshall discusses how she and Mrs. Clinton create a certain atmosphere for guests while Executive Chef Walter Scheib elaborates on the menu.

received programs and small American and Czech Republic flags to wave.

9:00 A.M.

Laura Schwartz and Carlos Elizondo, the protocol officer at Blair House, established radio contact to ensure that the timing of the Havels' entrance would be perfect. In the meantime, I met the President, the Vice President, and Mrs. Gore in the Map Room for a logistical briefing by Tom Groppel, the director of ceremonies and special events for the Military District of Washington.

9:25 A.M.

The President and I moved into position, while Carlos cued the Havels to depart for the White House. Exactly five minutes later, the President and I departed through the doors of the Diplomatic Reception Room to the South Lawn to *Ruffles and Flourishes* and *Hail to the Chief,* played by the U.S. Army Herald Trumpets lining the balcony above us, their brilliant brass catching the morning sun. The motorcade brought President Havel and Mrs. Havlová to the edge of the red carpet. Ambassador French welcomed them and we introduced them to the Vice President, the Secretary of State, and the Chairman of the Joint Chiefs of Staff.

The President then escorted President Havel to the reviewing stand while his wife, Dagmar, and I took our designated places. The scene was festive and regal, with the Honor Guard representing all five services of the military in formation according to seniority: Army, Marine Corps, Navy, Air Force, and Coast Guard. As the shots of the 21-gun salute faded, the Marine Band played the national anthem of the Czech Republic and then *The Star-Spangled Banner.*

9:55 A.M.

After reviewing the troops, the two heads of state delivered their first speeches, sharing their hopes that the visit would continue building strong relations between the two countries and extend peace and freedom throughout Eastern Europe. At the conclusion of the ceremony, we escorted our guests into the White House to the sounds of the Herald Trumpets. After the ceremony, we took the Havels to the Blue Room, where they signed the official guest book. We then proceeded to the Grand Foyer and greeted welcoming committees and delegations, who then joined a reception in the Blue Room.

10:30 A.M.

The President escorted President Havel to the West Wing for official meetings in the

Oval Office and Cabinet Room, and I invited Dagmar to our private residence for coffee. We talked about our families and the foundation she was starting to assist children. When we had finished, I asked White House Curator Betty Monkman to lead our guest on a special tour of the public rooms.

12:00 P.M.

President Havel departed for Blair House to meet his wife and go to the State Department, where the Vice President hosted a luncheon in their honor. After lunch, my husband joined President Havel for a joint press conference in the Dean Acheson Auditorium of the State Department. Then the Presidents parted until dinner.

Top: President Havel and President Clinton receive the evening's guests.
Bottom: Dr. and Mrs. Henry Kissinger were among the many distinguished guests.

Above: Secretary of State
Madeleine Albright, a
Czech native

4:00 P.M.

Capricia and I hosted a preview of the dinner for the press, with President Havel and Mrs. Havlová making a guest appearance at its conclusion. Mrs. Havlová is creating a botanical garden in her country, so I presented her with a small magnolia tree grown from a seedling of the oldest tree on the White House grounds, which was planted by President Andrew Jackson. I loved the idea that this historic magnolia's offsprings could take root in the soil of a new democracy like the Czech Republic. The Havels then returned to Blair House to get ready for the night's festivities.

Meanwhile, back at the White House, staff put the finishing touches on the State Dinner. As the hour neared, staff emerged in black tie, and members of the Marine Band put on their red military jackets and took their places to greet the guests with music.

6:45 P.M.

As the President and I dressed for dinner upstairs, our guests began arriving at the East Portico. Military personnel stepped forward to open vehicle doors so everyone could proceed directly into the East Wing, where each person was welcomed by Tutti Fairbanks and other Social Office

At the White House, there was little on anyone's mind except preparing for our 160 dinner guests. Walter and Roland had been at work for hours, cooking, decorating plates, and making preparations to ensure the dinner service would run smoothly. Assistant Usher Daniel Shanks worked with Maître d' George Hannie and the butlers to set tables in the East Room, making certain that no detail was left unattended—even checking that each place setting was equal in size to the next. The florists began arranging the centerpieces on the table with flowers that had been forced so that their fullest bloom would be at 8:30 that evening.

volunteers. As a flute trio played at the East Landing, guests checked their coats and were announced to the press gathered in the East Garden Room. People like Mia Farrow, Henry Kissinger, Stevie Wonder, Elie Wiesel, and Kurt Vonnegut—all personal friends of President Havel—were hastily jotted down by social reporters and occasionally stopped for an interview.

Calligraphers, stationed in the ground floor corridor, handed each guest an escort card, while music from a solo violinist filled the hall. Social aides, who are wonderfully adept at making everyone feel at home, escorted guests up the staircase to be introduced to the social secretary and brought to the State Dining Room for a reception.

7:00 P.M.

A direct telephone connection was established for Gary Walters, Laura Schwartz, and Carlos Elizondo to coordinate our timing with the Havels. At exactly 7:13, Laura cued Carlos to board the motorcade that would take the Havels to the North Portico.

7:15 P.M.

The President and I greeted President Havel and Mrs. Havlová, pausing so the

press could capture the first official photo of the evening. We guided them upstairs to join us for an intimate, pre-dinner gathering in the Yellow Oval Room. The top-ranking Czech officials joined Vice President and Mrs. Gore, Secretary of State Madeleine Albright, and our ambassadors for drinks and conversation. We took our guests out onto the Truman Balcony to enjoy the view, and the President provided one of his special tours of the Lincoln, Queens, and Treaty Rooms.

7:40 P.M.

Once Capricia received word that most of our guests had arrived, Ambassador French escorted our Yellow Oval Room guests, except President Havel and Mrs. Havlová, downstairs to join the State Dining Room reception. Capricia then explained to the Havels the protocol for the remainder of the evening.

7:45 P.M.

The Presidential Color Team, consisting of five very tall young men, representing each service, marched into the Yellow Oval and requested permission from the

Above: The President, the First Lady, President Havel, and Mrs. Havlová thank Lou Reed after his performance.

President to secure the colors, which means removing the American and presidential flags to be carried down to the foyer for the receiving line.

7:50 P.M.

The Marine Band played *Hail to the Chief* while we proceeded down the Grand Staircase, where we were announced and paused for the second official photo. Then we greeted each of our guests in the receiving line and introduced them to President Havel and Mrs. Havlová.

8:35 P.M.

After everyone was seated for dinner, the four of us were announced into the East Room. My husband offered a toast and tribute to the Czech Republic, sharing some of his favorite memories of President Havel—including the time Havel presented a personally inscribed tenor saxophone to my husband and "forced" him to play. President Havel offered his own thoughts about our countries' relationship and then presented the President with the Order of the White Lion, in honor of Bill's contributions to the welfare of the Czech Republic, Europe, and the world. He said, very simply, "Mr. President, the world needs you."

Opposite page: President Havel and Mrs. Clinton dance to the music of the Marine Band.

8:55 P.M.

On that inspirational note, dinner was served. We always split up couples at State Dinners to make conversation more interesting. President Havel and I enjoyed conversing with Mia Farrow, Mrs. Georgia Gilman (wife of Representative Benjamin Gilman), Lucy Calautti (Senator Byron Dorgan's chief of staff and wife of Senator Kent Conrad), Senators Ted Stevens and Carl Levin, Betsy Cohn (executive board member of the New Dramatist), Lewis Manilow (chairman of the Advisory Commission on Public Diplomacy), and Thomas Dine (president of Radio Free Europe). The President hosted Mrs. Havlová, Henry Kissinger, Kurt Vonnegut, Erica Sklar (wife of Eric Sklar, the president of Burrito Brothers), Senator Charles Hagel, Lee Clancey (mayor of Cedar Rapids), Representatives Norman Dicks and Pat Danner, and Marion Wiesel (vice president of the Elie Wiesel Foundation for Humanity).

9:50 P.M.

During dessert, the Marine Band Strolling Strings swept into the East Room and went from table to table, opening with a medley of *Beseda* and *Láska* by the Czech composer Leoš Janáček.

10:15 P.M.

After dinner was complete, Lou Reed stepped onto the stage, accompanied by the legendary Czech musician and former dissident, guitarist Milan Hlavsa. Their rousing performance still lingers along with the sound of the heartfelt applause at the end of the dinner. No one enjoyed the evening more than President Havel, who thanked me enthusiastically.

TBD P.M.

On the scenarios in our briefing books, the last entry denoting our departure time is always TBD—to be determined. After we thank our entertainers, protocol calls for us to escort our guests to their cars and bid them farewell. At that point, tradition dictates that the first couple returns inside for 15 minutes of dancing in the Grand Foyer. Here Bill and I frequently dispense with protocol and stay with our guests long into the night.

At the Havel dinner, however, when the Marine Dance Band struck up *Runaround Sue* as we were heading out the door, President Havel said he wanted to dance! So the four of us stayed to dance in the Grand Foyer, finally able to lose track of the time that had to be accounted for so carefully during the day.

CELEBRATING AMERICAN ARTS AND CULTURE

Above: Violist Nokuthula Ngwenyama performs at the 10th anniversary of National Public Radio's "Performance Today" in November 1997. Opposite page: In the shadow of the White House, Phil Driscoll gives a powerful trumpet solo in June 1998.

Our family, which includes a saxophone player (Bill), a dance fan (Chelsea), and one tone-deaf lover of music (me), has always loved and supported the arts in all forms. So you can imagine what a privilege it has been for us to enjoy and share with the world some of the best art and artists of all time.

One of my favorite paintings in the White House is the Gilbert Stuart portrait of George Washington—not only because of its colors and composition, but also because of what Dolley Madison did to save it. On a hot August day in 1814 during the War of 1812, she received word that the British were advancing and would soon invade Washington. She only had time to rescue the portrait and a few other items before fleeing the British forces, which captured the White House and burned it to the ground. When the house was rebuilt, the portrait Dolley saved was returned and now hangs in the East Room.

Above: The October 1996 presentation of Sand Dunes at Sunset, Atlantic City by Henry Ossawa Tanner, the first painting by an African-American artist to be represented in the White House collection.

Right: Mrs. Clinton and Social Secretary Ann Stock admire a piece created for the White House crafts collection by Bennett Bean. The bowl is white earthenware and gold leaf, pit-fired and painted. It features abstract design fragments of the American flag.

Dolley Madison understood what every first family must—that we are defined as a nation not just by laws, but by our music, paintings, sculptures, dance, and crafts. The White House is the oldest permanent venue for the arts in America, and we have been determined to continue that tradition by showcasing the great diversity of our creative expression, past and present.

Fine and Decorative Arts

Many people are familiar with the portraits of the Presidents and First Ladies that hang throughout the White House, but in fact, the permanent collection of fine arts is made up of more than 450 works in different genres.

Each work is carefully chosen by the Committee for the Preservation of the White House with one requirement: none of the artists can be living. (Except, of course, for the artists chosen to paint Presidential and First Lady portraits.) Because the works in the White House collection tell our story as a nation— from that Gilbert Stuart portrait of George Washington to Frederic Remington's western sculptures—I was eager to help fill some important gaps.

There was, for example, no painting by an African-American, an omission noticed by Mr. Edward Bell, an administrator at the State University of New York at New Paltz, who wrote in a letter to the President after visiting the White House in 1994:

> *I implore you to think about the impact that a tour of the White House has on African-American children, who travel great distances to see the home of our President, only to have it reinforced that they are invisible in many areas of America's glorious history.*

The President passed the letter on to me. And in the spring of 1994, I talked with the preservation committee, the endowment committee, and experts on African-American art to look for a work to add to the White House collection. Children of all races and backgrounds who visit the Green Room can now see *Sand Dunes at Sunset, Atlantic City,* by the noted 19th-century painter Henry Ossawa Tanner, whose mother's family had been slaves.

Visitors will also see Georgia O'Keeffe's *Bear Lake, New Mexico,* a painting evocative of the southwest region she loved so much. It is the collection's first work by a 20th-century woman artist to be exhibited in the public rooms. Now the O'Keeffe and the Tanner hang alongside works by John Singer Sargent, George Caleb Bingham, and other celebrated artists.

Above: Georgia O'Keeffe's painting Bear Lake, New Mexico *hangs in the Green Room. It is the first painting by a contemporary woman artist to hang on the State Floor.*

The White House also owns many decorative arts pieces that are vivid reminders of the lives of past occupants. President and Mrs. James Monroe's gilded objects, Mary Todd Lincoln's Victorian selections of the 1860s, and the Colonial Revival furnishings made for Theodore and Edith Roosevelt are still used in the State Dining Room.

Working with the Committee for the Preservation of the White House I was pleased to accept several important historical objects for the White House, including a pair of 18th-century mahogany chairs from the first President's house that were purchased for George Washington in 1789. Beautiful pieces of French porcelain from John and Abigail Adams's family service, acquired in 1998, bring to mind the first occupants of the President's house. Among the many documentary drawings and prints of the White House added during our years, I was especially delighted with the acquisition of an 1860 drawing of the Blue Room that came from the sale of Jacqueline Kennedy Onassis's possessions in 1994. These objects speak of the past and connect us with those who have lived here during the past 200 years.

The White House Collection of American Crafts

In many ways, the 19th-century decorative art objects owned by the White House were the crafts of their day, and it struck me that the Year of American Craft—1993, my husband's first year in office—presented an opportunity to celebrate their modern counterparts.

From handmade pots to colorful wall hangings, American crafts are an expression of our diverse regions and the aspirations of the people who inhabit them. Many First Ladies have taken an interest in American craft. Ellen Wilson decorated the private residence with weavings from Tennessee and the Carolinas. Eleanor Roosevelt furnished rooms with woodcrafts from Val-Kill Industries, the small workshop she founded in her hometown of Hyde Park, New York. Rosalynn Carter used the work of contemporary crafts artists instead of White House china at a luncheon for Senate spouses, with each table highlighting the work of a different potter, glassblower, or metalsmith.

So Social Secretary Ann Stock and I felt in good company when we decided to mount an exhibit of contemporary American crafts. With the help of the Smithsonian's Renwick Gallery Curator Michael Monroe and the advice of Joan Mondale, who is herself a ceramist, we put 72 magnificent objects on display in public rooms throughout the house.

People who walked through the White House that year were treated to pieces as varied as Ronald Fleming's intricately carved redwood bowl in the Red Room and David Levi's whimsical blue-and-yellow glass *Bird Jar* atop the marble-topped Monroe table in the Blue Room. Millions more have viewed the crafts collection as it tours museums across the country.

The Sculpture Garden

I have always loved sculpture and its inventive use of rock, metal, wood, glass, and other materials that surround us. In fact, on my first date with Bill Clinton we took a long walk that brought us to the Yale University Art Gallery in New Haven, where a Mark Rothko exhibit was featured and pieces by Henry Moore graced the sculpture garden. When we tried to go in-

side, we found the museum was closed. Bill persuaded the janitor to let us in after we promised to help pick up debris around the garden. (The rest, of course, is history.)

Shortly after we moved into the White House, I discovered there were very few sculptures in its collection. That seemed a notable oversight, and so I became committed to bringing sculpture to the White House for our millions of visitors and guests.

I turned to J. Carter Brown, the former director of the National Gallery of Art, and designer Kaki Hockersmith for help in creating an outdoor sculpture garden. The first question was: Where? One of my favorite places on the White House grounds is the Jacqueline Kennedy Garden, along

Below: Deputy Press Secretary Neel Lattimore and Mrs. Clinton confer before guests arrive at an exhibition reception in September 1997. Sculptures from left to right: Untitled *by Joel Shapiro, on loan from the National Gallery of Art;* Great Rock of Inner Seeking *by Isamu Noguchi, also on loan from the National Gallery; and* Agricola I *by David Smith, on loan from the Hirshhorn Museum and Sculpture Garden.*

the East Wing, whose alcoves seemed perfect places to feature outdoor sculpture that would be clearly visible to anyone walking through the glass-enclosed colonnade connecting the East Wing and the ground floor.

The second question was: What should we display? We wanted to feature works by contemporary American artists, and so we decided to stage a series of exhibits, organized around specific themes and overseen by the White House curators. Once our plan was approved by an enthusiastic Committee for the Preservation of the White House, J. Carter Brown took the idea to the Association of Art Museum Directors. Working together, we agreed to include sculpture only from public collections, and decided that each of the first four exhibits would represent a different region of the country.

Left: The Jacqueline Kennedy Garden is used for rotating exhibitions of sculpture. In the foreground is Hina *by Deborah Butterfield, a bronze on loan from the Modern Art Museum of Fort Worth for Exhibit III, mounted in 1995 and featuring art from the south and southwest regions. In the center is the snow-covered* Decoy *by Martin Puryear, on loan from the Los Angeles County Museum of Art. On the right is* Exhaling Pearls *by Joseph Havel, on loan from the Museum of Fine Art in Houston.*

Each exhibit's curator thought long and hard about the selection of individual pieces, considering not just the theme, but the scale and aesthetics of the group as a whole. We tried to place the works so visitors to the White House would see them to their best advantage. Large pieces such as Deborah Butterfield's life-sized bronze horses, *Willy, Argus, and Lucky,* fit well in the open space at the ends of the garden, while smaller pieces, such as Louise Bourgeois's *Black Flames,* neatly filled the alcoves.

The first exhibit, which opened on a beautiful fall day in 1994, taught all of us a great deal about what it takes to mount complex exhibits that include sometimes large and unwieldy artistic pieces.

For each installation, a large crane had to be moved into the garden to hoist the works onto their designated sites. We held our breaths as we watched John Scott's *Target I* lowered onto a concrete pedestal and as Alexander Calder's *Nenuphar* took its place as the anchor of the fifth exhibit.

Some pieces required a little more work because of their weight or height. To install Isamu Noguchi's seven-ton basalt *Great Rock of Inner Seeking* and George Rickey's 35-foot tall *Two Lines Oblique, Atlanta,* we had to dig huge underground footings beneath their pedestals.

Right: Painted steel *Nenuphar* by Alexander Calder, on loan from the National Museum of American Art, Smithsonian Institution, is admired by many guests at this September 1997 reception.

Far right: At a May 1995 reception, Mrs. Clinton with *Untitled* by Joel Shapiro, on loan from the National Gallery of Art.

Left: Washington writer Sarah Booth Conroy views an enlarged cast of *The Thinker* by Auguste Rodin, on loan from the Iris and B. Gerald Cantor Foundation.

Please respond to
The Social Secretary
THE WHITE HOUSE
at your earliest convenience
giving date of birth
AND
social security number
202-456-7787

Mrs. Clinton
requests the pleasure of your company
at a reception to celebrate
Twentieth Century American Sculpture
Inspired by French Sculptor,
Auguste Rodin
to be held at
The White House
on Friday, November 6, 1998
at nine-thirty o'clock

Visitor Entrance

Above: The invitation and reply card to the reception for the 1998 exhibition, "Twentieth Century American Sculpture at the White House: Inspired by Auguste Rodin."

Above: Windsong III, 1989 *by Robert Mangold, on loan from the Museum of Outdoor Arts, part of the eighth exhibit entitled "The View from Denver."*

Then there were issues most museums never have to consider. For one, the Secret Service needed to examine every piece before it could be placed in the garden. And we had to think about the impact of the blustery winds that kick up on the South Lawn whenever the President's helicopter lands or takes off.

Although dozens of museums have been involved in choosing and lending pieces, none of them alone could have covered the expense involved in mounting an entire exhibit. For that, we turned to one of this country's most important arts patrons—and our dear friend—Iris Cantor.

The Iris and B. Gerald Cantor Foundation underwrote the cost of seven exhibitions, including *Inspired by Rodin;* an exhibition of Native American sculpture was funded by the Heard Museum of Phoenix, Arizona. The *Rodin* exhibit displayed castings of *The Three Shades* and *The Thinker,* lent by Iris herself, along with nine related works by American artists who were influenced by Rodin.

It's amazing to think that since that first exhibit opened back in 1994, more than 10 million visitors have walked past the Sculpture Garden. They have been treated to American masterpieces such as George Segal's *Walking Man* and Alexander Calder's *Five Rudders.* They have enjoyed works by Georgia O'Keeffe, Willem de Kooning, Roy Lichtenstein, Isamu Noguchi, and Allan Houser, and they have viewed one of the few exhibitions of Native American sculpture ever mounted in the United States. The outpouring of appreciation has been overwhelming. Tourists frequently tell our guides how much they appreciate viewing this wonderful art while waiting to see the state rooms.

I know how they feel. I often find myself going out of my way to walk through the garden during the day. Each time, I feel energized by the spirit of those who spend their lives adding beauty to our surroundings and freeing our imaginations. And I am grateful for the role that sculpture plays in my own life—and the role I hope it will continue to play in the life of our nation.

Friends of Art and Preservation in Embassies

Whenever Bill and I visit another country, we always stop by the American Embassy to meet the men and women who represent us so well around the world. The minute we walk in the door, we immediately feel at home. This is especially true of those embassies that have been refurbished by or received art from the State Department's Art in Embassies program, and its private-sector partner, the Friends of Art and Preservation in Embassies (FAPE).

In our embassies and residences, we showcase all of America—not only our laws and treaties, but also our best art, architecture, and design. FAPE's work has

made it possible for us, and countless others, to see more than 3,000 American paintings, sculptures, decorative objects, and works of folk art in more than 200 of our embassies and residences abroad. Bill and I remember how pleased we were to walk into the Ambassador's Residence in Moscow and be greeted by Jasper Johns's *Two Flags,* or see Maurice Prendergast's *Maine, Blue Hills* making itself at home in our Paris embassy. In our New Delhi embassy, I saw Robert Rauschenberg's *Visual Autobiograph,* and on a blustery day at the new embassy in Ottawa, Canada, I had the opportunity to dedicate *Conjunction,* a 40-foot bronze sculpture by Joel Shapiro that celebrates the friendship between our nations.

Above: A study in black and white on the South Portico, May 1998.

Left: Chuck Close presents one of his portraits to the President and First Lady as Lee Annenberg looks on. Below: The President, First Lady, and Dorothy Lichtenstein at the presentation of a painting by Roy Lichtenstein.

FAPE was founded in 1986 by Lee Annenberg, Carol Price, Wendy Luers, and Lee Kimche McGrath. Several of their husbands had been ambassadors, and they had seen firsthand how our embassies—including the art on their walls—shape impressions of America around the world.

After all, our art is one of the best ambassadors America has.

Since its creation, FAPE has raised more than $10 million in private donations, in-kind contributions, and works of art. For many years, we held a reception followed by a black tie event to thank the people who make FAPE's work possible. For the first several years the event was held at the State Department, but in 1998 we decided to hold the first FAPE Gala at the White House.

Artists, patrons, and supporters of FAPE gathered in a pavilion on the South Lawn. Each table had a Tiffany bowl filled with peonies. The guests were treated to a superb meal of poached lobster, pepper-seared lamb, red and yellow tomato salad, and ice cream encased in thin white chocolate.

That night, FAPE announced its Millennium Gift to the nation, a promise to collect 200 works of contemporary art, and install them in U.S. embassies and residences around the world during the year 2000.

I was especially touched by the many tributes to Roy Lichtenstein, who had passed away only eight months before. His wife, Dorothy, donated his *Reflections on Senorita 1990* to FAPE. Artist Chuck Close unveiled his latest contribution, a print entitled *Roy,* which celebrated Lichtenstein. In fact, when I went to Holland the following year, I took the print on the plane with me and personally delivered it to the ambassador.

When I think about the role that FAPE has played in three administrations, Republican and Democrat, I remember something Bill said during that gala in 1998: "Every time someone walks into an American embassy anywhere in the world, I want them to see that we are many people, we are many religions, we are many races but we believe that what unites us is far greater than what divides us."

That is what we wish for the future—a world where the creative spirit may be freely expressed, celebrated for its uniqueness, and cherished for its contribution to our common humanity.

Above: Peonies grace the center of a table at the May 1998 dinner for the Friends of Art and Preservation in Embassies.

Above: Mickey Mangun and the Messiah Singers from Alexandria, Louisiana. Mangun sang at the inaugural church services for President Clinton in 1993 and 1997. Below: President Clinton participates in a musical moment at the 40th anniversary of the Newport Jazz Festival on June 18, 1993, held on the South Lawn.

In Performance at the White House

For our family, one of the great pleasures of living in the White House has been the opportunity to bring the best performers in America to one of the best known stages in America. On any given day, the talent in the East Room or the tented performance space on the South Lawn can rival the top concert halls, opera houses, and theaters in America.

Of course, for the entertainers, there is no marquee with their name in lights. The only compensation is a world-class meal or a private tour of the White House.

I yet marvel at the range of artists who have performed at the White House during our eight years. The list includes Itzhak Perlman, Rita Moreno, Wynton Marsalis, Liza Minnelli, Leonard Slatkin, Tony Bennett, Mary Chapin Carpenter, Yo-Yo Ma, Lionel Hampton, and Mandy Patinkin. We've also had pianist Van Cliburn, who has performed for every President since Harry Truman.

The first time a concert was broadcast live by radio was when Mrs. Kennedy brought Pablo Casals to the White House in 1961. Mrs. Nixon hosted a number of musical presentations for guests in the East Room, and Mrs. Carter joined with WETA, the public broadcasting affiliate in Washington, D.C., to create the televised *In Performance at the White House* program.

Before Bill became President, we watched memorable performances by Vladimir Horowitz, Leontyne Price, and Mikhail Baryshnikov on television. As soon as we arrived, I hoped we could increase the number of WETA performances broadcast to the American people. I turned to my friend Sharon Rockefeller, the president of WETA. Together we envisioned programs that would appeal to a broad range of musical tastes, spanning generations and genres. Since then, we have featured blues, dance, gospel, country, musicals, cabaret, and everything in between.

Our first concert was "A Salute to the Newport Jazz Festival," in 1993, which featured legends such as Joe Henderson and Rosemary Clooney, as well as younger stars like Bobby McFerrin. In the closing segment, Bill, having listened all night to some of his favorite music and musicians, couldn't resist any longer. He picked up a saxophone and joined in.

All the shows had memorable moments. I loved hearing Aretha Franklin belt out classics like *Respect* and *Ol' Man River*. But it was her rendition of *Tobacco Road* with Lou Rawls that got the most attention. They were about to start singing when they realized pianist Les McCann wasn't on stage. No matter. Aretha Franklin and Lou Rawls improvised their own boogie-woogie bass line and kept right on going.

Above: CeCe Winans and her backup group rehearse for the WETA gospel performance in 1998.

Below: Gail West, spouse of Secretary of Veterans Affairs Togo West, the President, the First Lady, and the Reverend Jesse Jackson join hands and raise their voices in song.

Below left: CeCe Winans and the Morgan State University Choir brought the guests to their feet.

The President is always involved in these programs, but never more so than with the celebration of gospel music. He grew up with the music and it has always played a central role in his life. For the WETA gospel performance, he personally chose CeCe Winans and many of the other singers, whom he has known for years. He helped put together the program and even sat in on rehearsals.

When the night came, the pavilion had hanging cutouts designed to look like windows in a church, and everything in the pavilion—flowers, linens, and china—was white. The audience was made up of people of all religious backgrounds, singing, chanting, holding hands, and enjoying themselves to the fullest—and no one more so than my husband.

Above: Aaron Neville and Linda Ronstadt sing a moving duet in May 1996. Top right: At the VH1 Concert of the Century (from left to right): Lenny Kravitz, Sheryl Crow, Al Greene, and B.B. King. Bottom right: The President thanks the night's entertainers at WETA's In Performance production of "The Blues," in July 1999. Performers included Della Reese and Jonny Lang.

Concert of the Century

I don't think the South Lawn has ever rocked and rolled the way it did on October 23, 1999, when Bill and I joined hundreds of guests for the concert of the century. Under a huge pavilion, the musicians were introduced by an all-star ensemble, including Gwyneth Paltrow, Meryl Streep, and Robert De Niro. Garth Brooks sang *American Pie,* Gloria Estefan and 'N Sync teamed up with the East Harlem Violin Project to perform *Music of the Heart,* and Al Green sank to his knees, singing the civil rights anthem *A Change Is Gonna Come.*

When Kevin Spacey introduced B. B. King, he was right in saying, "the thrill is not gone." B. B. King played electrifying sets with Lenny Kravitz, Melissa Etheridge, and Eric Clapton. He even patted Clapton on the back, saying, "You get better all the time, young man."

All of us were there to support music education in our schools. The concert was co-sponsored by the National Endowment for the Arts and produced by VH1's Save the Music Foundation, which has donated thousands of musical instruments to schools where band and orchestra programs have been eliminated or cut back. This concert was part of a campaign that I have waged to put the arts and music back into our classrooms and our children's lives. The performers at the concert spoke about the role that music education had played in their lives. My husband even remarked that he wouldn't be President today were it not for his school music classes and band experiences. As I have traveled to schools around the country, I have seen the power of the arts not only to spark a child's confidence and creativity—but also to keep students from dropping out or giving up. I have met

Below: Savion Glover and NYOT (Not Your Ordinary Tappers) tap their way through a rehearsal in March 1998.

Above: Mrs. Clinton and award-winning actress Meryl Streep before the VH1 concert, October 1999.

Below: Gloria Estefan and 'N Sync perform the theme from the movie Music of the Heart at the VH1 Save the Music Concert.

children who joined an orchestra instead of a gang, children who had never spoken until they took an art class, and children who have picked up a paintbrush or instrument to follow their dreams. Every child deserves that opportunity.

For three glorious hours on the South Lawn, some of the best musicians in America played their hearts out so that all our children might have the chance to do the same.

Millennium Evenings

On February 11, 1998, Bernard Bailyn, a Pulitzer prize–winning historian and Harvard professor emeritus, was the featured speaker at the first of our Millennium Evenings. He delivered a moving and funny lecture about the birth of our American ideals, and how hard we must still work to live up to them. The evening was a perfect beginning to a program my husband and I had been planning for years.

As Bill and I talked about the coming turn of the century and the beginning of the new millennium, we wanted to "honor the past and imagine the future" by exploring the ideas, arts, culture, and science that have defined our people and country. We decided to create the White House Millennium Council to realize our vision and asked my then Deputy Chief of Staff Ellen McCulloch-Lovell to head it up.

We asked Ellen and her staff to organize a series of Millennium Evenings that would highlight the creativity and inventiveness of the American people. We chose to feature leading scholars, creators, and visionaries through this series, which meant that, on any given Millennium Evening, we might end up with the greatest number of poets, physicists, jazz musicians, women's historians, or geneticists ever to assemble in the White House.

We also knew that we wanted to open these evenings up to as many citizens as possible, and the East Room, even tightly packed, only has room for about 300 chairs. So we turned to technology—more specifically, to Sun Microsystems to help create satellite downlinks and the first ever cybercast event from the White House. Through the miracle of e-mail, we took questions from people all over the world during the actual event, making each evening a truly interactive global experience.

I had a computer monitor next to me on the stage, where I could read the questions; the first question was from Everett in North Dakota, who was virtually in the room with the President, Professor Bailyn, and me. That was also true of all the community college students at satellite downlink sites around the country and people watching on C-SPAN.

The Millennium Evenings, which are sponsored by the National Endowment for the Humanities, explore topics from the meaning of the millennium itself to new discoveries "Under the Sea, Beyond the Stars."

One particularly memorable evening in September 1998 featured Wynton Marsalis and Marian McPartland leading a musical tour of jazz, illustrating how this uniquely American art form reflects our democracy. This event, which included a 17-piece jazz band playing on a special stage, was broadcast live on VH1 and cybercast so that people from everywhere could hear that musical expression of our democractic values.

We were honored to have President Václav Havel of the Czech Republic in the audience that night—his presence, as a leader in the fight for democracy in his own country, made the experience even more meaningful.

In April 1998, National Poetry Month, Poet Laureate Robert Pinsky and former Laureates Robert Haas and Rita Dove joined my husband and me to celebrate American poetry. The three of them stood together, reading selections by some of our greatest American poets, including Emily Dickinson, Robert Frost, and Wallace Stevens. Instead of our traditional welcome, I opened the evening by reading Howard Nemerov's *The Makers,* and Bill closed the program with Ralph Waldo Emerson's *Concorde Hymn.*

The President and Mrs. Clinton request the pleasure of your company at a Millennium Lecture to be held at

The White House

on Friday, September 18, 1998 at seven o'clock

Above: An invitation to "Jazz: An Expression of Democracy," the fourth Millennium Evening, held in September 1998.

But it wasn't just the famous poets who stole the show. Robert Pinsky's Favorite Poem Project recorded Americans from all walks of life reading their favorite poems and explaining why they were meaningful. We invited some of these citizens to the White House that night.

A seventh-grade girl from Washington, D.C., offered a spirited and touching rendition of Langston Hughes's *Life Is Fine.* A minister from Boston told how, as a young, rebellious man in high school, he had been taken under the wing of a teacher who introduced him to the poetry that got him off the streets. When he read one of those poems, Henry Wadsworth Longfellow's *Psalm of Life,* we were deeply moved. And when a disabled veteran in a wheelchair read, with a deep, gravelly voice, Robert Frost's *Stopping by Woods on a Snowy Evening,* we could all sense how these words kept him going despite all his obstacles. He, too, had miles to go before he slept.

Right: "The Living Past: Commitments for the Future," with Bernard Bailyn, was the first Millennium Evening. Held in the East Room in February 1998, it was the first event ever cybercast from the White House.

We also celebrated with Professor Stephen Hawking the spirit of discovery that has shaped human history over the last millennium. In March 1998, he took us in his wheelchair from the East Room to the cosmos and back, and he did it all with a computer, communicating by selecting words from a screen. The computer then produces a voice, which he jokingly says sounds somewhat Irish.

This series of discussions has looked not only at our proudest accomplishments, but also at our greatest failures. No one made a sound in the East Room in April 1999, as Holocaust survivor and Nobel prize recipient Elie Wiesel spoke eloquently about "The Perils of Indifference" in the face of a horror like the Holocaust, the worst chapter in the bloodstained 20th century. He then took part in a discussion about the hatred and indifference that still plague us today.

Under any circumstances, this would have been a powerful evening, but it took on even more meaning when it happened to coincide with the events taking place in Kosovo.

That night, the President spoke about our moral obligation to take a stand against ethnic cleansing in Kosovo. A Rwandan woman in the audience described how her family barely escaped slaughter, and asked how the murderers and their victims are now supposed to live together as neighbors. And finally a priest asked how, given the bloodshed of the past century, we can continue to have hope. Elie Wiesel answered, "What choice do we have? If we don't have hope, we must invent it."

Optimism about the future filled the East Room in October 1999, when scientists Vinton Cerf, Senior Vice President of Internet Architecture and Technology for MCI WorldCom, and Eric Lander, Director of the Whitehead Institute/MIT Center for Genome Research, explained how the revolution in computer technology made

Above: A question for the evening comes across the Internet.

possible the revolution in genetics, and how both are transforming our lives. These advances will lead to changes in everything, from the creation of a refrigerator that will order our food to a cure for Alzheimer's disease.

Professor Lander stunned us with the revelation that, despite all our differences—race, religion, ethnicity, or gender—all human beings have 99.9 percent of the same DNA. Bill and I have talked about that fact ever since. Think about all the bloodshed, violence, and hatred generated by that one-tenth of one percent.

There have to be ways, as we enter this new millennium, for us to celebrate the 99.9 percent we have in common. And that is what we hope these Millennium Evenings have helped Americans to do.

Top: Dr. Stephen Hawking lectures at the second Millennium Evening, "Imagination and Change: Science in the Next Millennium."
Left: Elie Wiesel speaks at the seventh Millennium Evening, "The Perils of Indifference: Lessons Learned from a Violent Century," in April 1999.

The Pritzker Prize

On June 17, 1998, Bill and I joined many of the world's finest architects to present the 20th Pritzker Architecture Prize to Renzo Piano, an Italian architect whose extraordinary designs can be found all over the globe—from the Centre Georges Pompidou in Paris to the Kansai Air Terminal in Osaka, Japan.

That night, we all dined in a tented pavilion on the South Lawn, in full sight of three of the greatest pieces of American architecture—the Jefferson Memorial, the Washington Monument, and the White House. We then listened to distinguished architectural historian Vincent Scully describe how what we build reflects who we are.

For 20 years, the Pritzker Prize, the most prestigious award in architecture, has honored the people whose buildings lift our sights and fill our surroundings with beauty. The prize is named for the late Jay A. Pritzker and his wife, Cindy, whose family generously supports art and architecture. To date seven Americans have been honored, including Robert Venturi, Kevin Roche, and I. M. Pei, all of whom were there that night.

This international award is presented in significant buildings like the Château of

Above: Classical columns set an elegant tone for the dinner at the Pritzker Prize dinner, June 17, 1998.

Right: The program for the Pritzker Prize dinner.

Far right: Guests descend the stairs of the South Portico to enter the pavilion on the South Lawn. In front, award-winning architect and designer of the Vietnam Veterans Memorial Maya Lin is accompanied by her husband, Daniel Wolf.

PROGRAM

Opening Remarks
MRS. CLINTON

Remarks
J. CARTER BROWN
Chairman, The Pritzker Architecture Prize Jury

VINCENT SCULLY
Sterling Professor Emeritus of the History of Art
Yale University

JAY AND CINDY PRITZKER
Founders of The Pritzker Architecture Prize

RENZO PIANO
1998 Pritzker Laureate

Closing Remarks
THE PRESIDENT

Left: I. M. Pei and friends. Mr. Pei, who received the Pritzker in 1983, designed such American landmarks as Boston's John F. Kennedy Library.

Left: The South Portico
Below: Wisteria adorns
the railing.

Versailles in France, the Prague Castle in the Czech Republic, and the White House, which celebrated its 200th birthday in November 2000.

The architect of the White House, selected by George Washington, was James Hoban, from Ireland. He entered the contest in 1792 to design the President's house. He beat out some very tough competition, including Thomas Jefferson, who had designed the contest and had submitted an anonymous entry.

Hoban didn't create a castle towering above a kingdom. Instead, he designed a graceful building that came to symbolize our democracy—simple and strong, beautiful and open to all.

Kennedy Center Honors

One of the most magical and memorable occasions of every year is the night we pay tribute to the recipients of the Kennedy Center Honors. It's a tradition for this ceremony to be the first event that we hold in the East Room after the Christmas decorations are up, and there's no better way to kick off the holiday season.

Every year, the Kennedy Center recognizes five Americans for their significant contributions to the worlds of dance, music, theater, opera, movies, and television. It is one of the highest honors a performing artist can receive in America.

Below: Willie Nelson, André Previn, and Shirley Temple Black are escorted to the East Room to receive recognition from the President and Mrs. Clinton.

Since President Jimmy Carter helped launch the Kennedy Center Honors in 1978, a White House reception for the honorees has been an integral part of the Kennedy Center's weekend-long celebration.

On that night, Washington comes together, not as Democrats or Republicans, cabinet secretaries or senators, but as fans of the performing arts. The White House is aglow, not just with Christmas lights but with the energy generated by some of our most gifted and beloved artists. Before a black-tie, standing-room-only audience in the East Room, the President offers a personal salute to each honoree, who over the years have included comedian Bill Cosby, conductor Sir Georg Solti, ballerina Maria Tallchief, and country singer Johnny Cash.

After the White House reception, Bill and I attend the gala at the Kennedy Center Opera House, where the honorees are saluted by performers and colleagues who have been touched in some way by their work. "The Boss," Bruce Springsteen, once serenaded Bob Dylan with a rendition of *The Times They Are A-Changing*. David Letterman recited one of his hilarious top-ten lists for Johnny Carson. And no one who was there will forget the all-star cast of blues musicians, from Bonnie Raitt to Dr.

Left: Bill Cosby passes a note to Fred Ebb. Mr. Cosby was honored for his comic genius. Mr. Ebb was honored for his work with John Kander, with whom he has the longest running partnership in Broadway musical history. Above: A card listing the honorees accompanied the invitation.

Left: Honorees in 1997 included (from left to right): Edward Villella, Jessye Norman, Charlton Heston, Bob Dylan, and Lauren Bacall.

John, who brought the house down with a jam session in honor of B. B. King.

The Kennedy Center is just one of the many cultural institutions the President and I have supported and showcased in Washington. We have hosted tributes and receptions, and attended performances at Ford's Theater, the Washington Opera, the National Symphony Orchestra, and the Folger Shakespeare Library.

We have done all this because we believe that the arts are not a luxury but a necessary and vital part of American life. During the darkest days of the Civil War, Abraham Lincoln often visited the theater, and he ordered work to go forward on the Capitol dome. Franklin Roosevelt, in the midst of World War II, dedicated the National Gallery of Art in Washington. As President Kennedy said, "these leaders understood that the life of the arts, far from being an interruption, a distraction in the life of a nation, is very close to the center of a nation's purpose and is a test of the quality of a nation's civilization."

Every day of the past eight years, the President and I have tried to meet that test—in the performances we've hosted, the art we've showcased, the institutions we've supported, and the historic commitment to the arts we have tried to keep alive in America's house.

Above left: Actor and choreographer Geoffrey Holder and his wife, ballet dancer Carmen DeLavallade.
Above right: Sir Georg Solti conducts members of the Marine Band in December 1993.

Above: The President and First Lady, and Vice President and Mrs. Gore greet Johnny Carson at the June 1994 reception.

Left: Lauren Bacall and the First Lady exchange greetings at the 1997 reception.

"*A nation reveals itself not only by the people it produces,*
but also by the people it honors."

—*President John F. Kennedy*

Above: Team captains Julie
Foudy and Carla Overbeck
present President Clinton
with his own team shirt
at the 1999 South Lawn
celebration of America's
Women's World Cup
champions.
Opposite page: SSgt Tage
Larsen of "The President's
Own," the Marine Band.

It was a hot and humid August day in Washington, not

exactly perfect weather for an outdoor event on the South

Lawn. But nothing could have kept away the many fans and

admirers who joined Bill and me in congratulating the

Women's National Soccer Team on their 1999 World Cup

victory. There was, of course, one visible difference between

this crowd and others that have come to the White House to

celebrate championship teams: This audience was

dominated by young girls.

Fathers and mothers brought along their excited daughters.

Many were aspiring soccer stars awestruck at the prospect of

shaking hands with Mia Hamm, Julie Foudy, and the rest of

the superstars. Thanks to women like these, an entire generation of American girls now believe, "I can be an athlete or an artist, a scientist or a Supreme Court justice. I can be anything I want to be."

Over the past eight years, the President and I have been privileged to honor some of our country's greatest heroes at the annual Medal of Freedom ceremonies. While some recipients, like Bob Dole, are famous, others are activists who work tirelessly and anonymously behind the scenes. One, the late Marjorie Stoneman Douglas, was 103 when the President awarded her the medal for her conserva-

tion work, especially her fight to save the Florida Everglades. We would have understood if she had skipped the ceremony, but she was determined to be there. So, accompanied by a doctor and an assistant, she travelled from her home near Miami the day before and stayed with us at the White House to summon her strength for the moment onstage when she received her medal.

When Atlanta hosted the 1996 Summer Olympic Games, Chelsea and I had seen the torch lit in Olympia, Greece, months before the games began. So we were especially excited to invite thousands of

the community activists who had carried the torch to watch its arrival in Washington. Sister Mary Popit, who works with homeless women in our nation's capital, carried the flame high above her head as she arrived at the gate. Then, she handed it off to I. King Jordan, the first deaf president of Gallaudet University, the only liberal arts university for the deaf in the world. He took a lap around the South Lawn and then headed through a chute of onlookers to the cauldron. The flame, with all its symbolism, lit up the clear night just seconds before a torrential downpour drenched all of us—but did not extinguish the light!

Above: The departure ceremony for the Olympic torch took place on the South Lawn on June 21, 1996. The event was a celebration of the Olympic spirit and a tribute to the community heroes who carried the torch across America. Here, Washington, D.C., community hero Lang Brown makes his way up the South Lawn and out the gate as the torch resumes its journey.

Special Olympics

The Special Oympics was the creation of a special brand of American hero, the kind whose unshakable decency, humanity and, yes, stubbornness, helps turn seemingly insurmountable challenges into victories. I'm referring to Eunice Kennedy Shriver, sister of the late President John F. Kennedy and the wife of Sargent Shriver, the first director of the Peace Corps.

Eunice refused to accept the conventional wisdom of her day, which claimed that people with disabilities were incapable of leading active and productive lives. At a time when children with mental retardation were traditionally cloistered from the world, Eunice hosted summer camps in her backyard to give these children the chance to run, swim, play soccer, and ride horses.

From these fun-filled backyard competitions, the Special Olympics was born on July 20, 1968, at Soldier Field in Chicago. That first year, 1,000 athletes took part in the games. Today, more than 1.2 million Special Olympians in 165 countries train and compete around the world, shattering records and stereotypes, showing incredible courage and skills, and building the kind of confidence that will last a lifetime.

So when Eunice asked me to host a White House dinner to mark the 30th anniversary of the Special Olympics, the only possible answer was yes. From the outset, I was determined to make this dinner not only a celebration, but a way to spotlight the *abilities* of the 50 million people around the globe with mental retardation.

When the night of this elegant black-tie affair arrived, our guests came to a White House decked out in all its Christmas glory. The President, Eunice, Sarge, and I greeted everyone, then we boarded

Below: Vanessa Williams and Jon Bon Jovi serenade Special Olympics Global Messengers Billy Quick and Sophia Wesolowsky at the 30th anniversary celebration of the Special Olympics in December 1998.

Left: Special Olympics Global Messenger Michael Bojarski with Nadia Comaneci. Twelve global messengers were chosen to communicate the Special Olympics message to audiences worldwide.

Above: The Shriver grandchildren enjoy the evening.

Right: The anniversary dinner was held in a pavilion on the South Lawn.

trolleys to a large pavilion on the South Lawn where we had dinner and were treated to a special concert featuring Special Olympics supporters: Emcee Whoopi Goldberg, Eric Clapton, Mary J. Blige, Sheryl Crow, Jon Bon Jovi, Run-DMC, Tracy Chapman, and Vanessa Williams. A host of athletic heroes were on hand, from Olympic gold medal gymnast Nadia Comaneci to former heavyweight boxing champion Evander Holyfield.

The theme of the evening was "The Next Generation of Special Olympics Heroes."

We heard tributes to the countless Americans who encourage these athletes to reach for the stars, and the brave men and women who find the courage to compete. We heard moving stories of athletes who participated in past games and now serve as coaches and mentors. We met volunteers whose sons and daughters have taken up the cause, as well as a whole new generation of Shriver and Kennedy children for whom supporting the Special Olympics has become a way of life.

One of the most touching moments came when Special Olympian Loretta Claiborne, a veteran of the Boston Marathon, stepped to the podium. "Yes," she said, "kids called me names in school. They always told me what I couldn't do. But I had the chance to become part of something no one can take away from me, to become an athlete, to join a movement, to make a difference."

The Special Olympics helps all of us imagine a future in which every child can do that. Really, that is how it all started—in the backyard of one woman who believed she could make a difference, and inspired others to do the same. Eunice put it so well when she said, "As we hope for the best in them, hope is reborn in us."

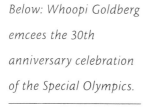

Below: Whoopi Goldberg emcees the 30th anniversary celebration of the Special Olympics.

Marine Band

"From the Halls of Montezuma to the shores of Tripoli . . . " I can still remember the words of the *Marines' Hymn,* which I learned as a little girl. Imagine, all these years later, what a thrill it is to hear the Marine Band play, especially at the Commanders-in-Chief dinner, where they perform for the entire military leadership. As the band performs the *Armed Forces Medley,* featuring the service songs of the Army, Navy, Marine Corps, Air Force, and Coast Guard, the chief of each respective branch proudly stands to offer a salute and sing along.

From its very first days in 1798, the Marine Band has accompanied the most celebratory and somber events in our history, from presidential inaugurations to the funeral of President Kennedy, where it expressed the heartfelt anguish of the nation.

During our time at the White House, members of "The President's Own," as the band has been called since the Jefferson administration, have witnessed extraordinary historic occasions such as the signing of the Middle East peace agreements. They have accompanied famous

Right: The day's music tucked in a hat.

entertainers, played for traditional events such as the annual Easter Egg Roll, and even serenaded us on our birthdays. So, on the occasion of the 200th anniversary of America's oldest professional music organization, there was no question that we would turn the tables and pay tribute to these talented men and women.

As Bill and I walked out onto the South Lawn on July 10, 1998, we were thrilled to see retired as well as current musicians, accompanied by proud family members. Under the direction of LtCol Timothy

Right: The invitation to the 200th-anniversary celebration of the Marine Band.

Below: The President, Mrs. Clinton, Gen Charles C. Krulak, and the Marine Band are announced to guests at the 200th anniversary of the Marine Band.

The Marine Band at the White House · July 16, 1921

Foley, the band entertained us with selections ranging from George Gershwin's *'S Wonderful* to the *Marines' Hymn.* Of course, no tribute would be complete without *Stars and Stripes Forever* by John Philip Sousa, who conducted the band from 1880 to 1892. It is Sousa's own gold-tipped baton, the band's most precious artifact, that Foley uses when he conducts.

My husband, the great music lover, is the band's most enthusiastic fan—and has been known, at times, to get up and sing or play along. During a State Dinner or some other performance, I might catch him tapping his toes to the beat, and I know that he is dying to trade places with one of the saxophonists. I remember a special night when MGySgt Charles Corrado was playing show tunes on the piano. Bill and I were listening and singing downstairs with our guests. Chelsea and her friends were dancing in and out of the rooms. Charlie's magic filled the entire White House. Bill often says that one of the things he will miss most when he leaves the White House is the music of the Marine Band. I couldn't agree more. We will miss their music, their service, and their spirit.

Above: SSgt Christopher E. Gayle and his daughter Yasmine
Left: The next generation: GySgt David A. Murray and his son Adam

Right: The band entertains the guests with a grand entrance, marching down the South Lawn.
Below: The Drum Major of the Marine Band has the sole honor of wearing this badge.

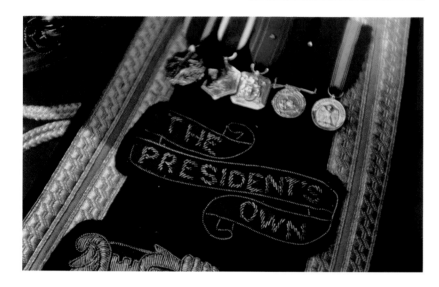

Arts and Humanities

For more than 200 years, American artists and thinkers representing the wide range of American culture have moved our hearts and souls. My husband and I have taken every opportunity to celebrate the central role that paintings, poetry, history, dance, music, literature, and all the rest of the arts and humanities have played in the lives of our citizens and country.

Ray Charles was one of the first people this administration chose to receive the National Medal of Arts, which honors outstanding contributions to the arts by American citizens. Since then, Bill has bestowed this award on artists as diverse as percussionist Tito Puente, actress Angela Lansbury, architect Frank Gehry, and sculptor George Segal. We have also recognized patrons and organizations such as the Juilliard School, which nurtured the voice of Leontyne Price, the violin of Itzhak Perlman, and the jazz of Wynton Marsalis.

The National Humanities Medal honors individuals or groups who improve our understanding of or access to the humanities. Our honorees have included

Garrison Keillor, of public radio's *A Prairie Home Companion,* filmmaker Steven Spielberg, Harvard African-American studies scholar Henry Louis "Skip" Gates, and Patricia Battin, whose Commission on Preservation and Access has helped save nearly one million "brittle books" for future generations.

Both Bill and I derive strength, solace, and inspiration from the arts. In 1995, when he found out that two saxophone quartets were scheduled to perform at the White House in conjunction with the arts and humanities festivities, he requested—and was granted—a short private concert. After admiring the musicians' instruments, he told them how much music had influenced his life.

My husband especially savors the moments when the recommendations for the arts and humanities awards cross his desk, because so many of these scholars and artists have touched our lives in very personal ways.

It was a special treat, for example, to single out children's author Maurice Sendak, as we remembered reading *Where the Wild Things Are* so many times when Chelsea was little that we practically knew it by heart. When the wife of actor

Opposite page: The New Century Saxophone Quartet gives a private recital for President Clinton in the East Room in October 1995.

Above: Mrs. Clinton greets Walter and Lee Annenberg at the 1993 ceremony dinner.

Above: The newly expanded National Medal of Arts and National Humanities Medal ceremony on the South Lawn in 1993.

and dancer Gene Kelly accepted his award, we both laughed at the memory of Bill imitating the famous soggy dance sequence from one of our favorite films, *Singin' in the Rain.* We both loved Gregory Peck's portrayal of the courageous Alabama lawyer Atticus Finch in *To Kill a Mockingbird,* and Bill particularly was influenced—as were a whole generation of young southerners—by William Styron's *The Confessions of Nat Turner.*

In earlier years, the arts and humanities medals were awarded at separate smaller events. When we arrived, we wanted to elevate the arts and humanities consistent with their importance to our nation. My

then Deputy Chief of Staff Melanne Verveer suggested that we expand the number of medalists and recognize these honorees in a much larger joint ceremony.

Bill and I agreed. We wanted to host an event as extraordinary as the talent it honors. At Melanne's suggestion, we moved the event to the South Lawn and were able to invite more than 1,000 guests, including family members of the honorees, prominent patrons and artists, and the dedicated staffs of the National Endowment for the Arts and the National Endowment for the Humanities. We also instituted a formal arts and humanities dinner that is now like a State Dinner.

The entertainment for these evenings often features talented young artists. When we honored the National Dance Institute's founder, Jacques D'Amboise, young performers, ranging in age from 5 to 16, danced in the aisles. And in one of the most memorable moments of our White House years, Leontyne Price, moved by the evening and the music of the Army's Strolling Strings ensemble at the 1993 dinner, stood at her table and treated us to an impromptu rendition of *Stardust.* Then baritone Robert Merrill followed suit by singing *(I'll Be Loving You) Always.* I was sitting with Ambassador Walter Annenberg, who exclaimed he had just seen the best performance of the year.

Below: Leontyne Price breaks into song at the 1993 dinner.

Left: Bob Hope received the Medal of Arts in 1995 for his contributions in the field of entertainment.

Below: The President speaks to guests and honorees at the 1994 dinner.

Left: The President, the First Lady, and Gregory Peck in 1998. Academy Award–winner Peck was twice appointed to the National Council on the Arts. Below: Ray Charles and the President at the 1993 morning ceremony. Mr. Charles was awarded the 1993 arts medal for his contributions to music and entertainment.

Top: Harry Belafonte and his wife, Julie, at the 1994 dinner.
Bottom: Honoree Itzhak Perlman and Dorothy Delay, his former teacher from the Juilliard School, October 1994.

Medals

Medal of Freedom recipient Barbara Jordan once said, "What the people want is very simple: They want an America as good as its promise." In many ways, our

Above: Vernon Baker received the Medal of Honor in 1997 for his heroic acts in World War II near Viareggio, Italy.

Medal of Freedom recipients, who are awarded the highest civilian honor bestowed by the government in recognition of contributions to peace and unity, are the guardians of America's promise. Just think of Dr. Martin Luther King Jr. and Supreme Court justices Thurgood Marshall and William Brennan.

Think of Fred Korematsu, who received the honor after waiting 30 years for the Supreme Court to overturn his conviction for failing to report for internment during World War II. Think of Cardinal Joseph Bernardin, who was recognized for being "a man of God and a man of the people," and of White House Press Secretary Jim Brady, who has used his own painful experience to keep handguns out of the hands of criminals.

These Americans—just like those who have been honored at the White House throughout history—show us that the most powerful job in any democracy is not otherwise president or prime minister, but citizen.

We have recognized lending institutions that nurture small businesses by offering microcredit loans, small loans to low-income men and women who might not otherwise qualify for traditional business financing. We have highlighted programs that use art to help at-risk youth stay on the right track in life. And we have honored diverse citizens from every sector of society who have, through the years, breathed real life into our values of justice, freedom, and equality.

The Medal of Honor is the highest military award given to a member of the armed forces of the United States for a deed of personal bravery or self-sacrifice above and beyond the call of duty. When Bill presented the medal to eight African-American World War II veterans in 1997, he righted one of the nation's greatest wrongs. More than one million African-Americans served in World War II, yet none received the nation's highest awards for bravery in battle. Seven of the eight recipients chosen had died before they could receive their award, but 77-year-old Vernon Baker traveled to the White House to receive his long-overdue honor from a grateful nation.

Baker was a second lieutenant in the all-black 92nd Infantry Division. He wiped out four German machine gun nests, drew fire on himself so wounded comrades could be evacuated, then led a battalion through enemy minefields. As he received his well-deserved medal, he said his military service and life were governed by a simple credo: "Remember the mission, set the example, keep going." All of us owe a debt of gratitude to Lieutenant Baker and all those like him who have shaped our history and strengthened our democracy.

Right: Medal of Honor winners Shizuya Hayashi, Barney Hajiro, and Rudolph Dazila, and President Clinton during a ceremony honoring Asian Americans who served in the American Armed Forces during World War II.

Sacagawea

Sacagawea was only 15 years old and six months pregnant when she set out to guide the Lewis and Clark expedition. Many historians believe that without her skills the mission wouldn't have succeeded. She knew several Indian languages and helped the explorers safely make their way from the northern Great Plains to the Pacific Ocean and back. She knew which plants were edible. She was a skilled navigator. And her presence with her newborn child signaled to Indian tribes that the Lewis and Clark party came in peace.

When the U.S. Mint announced that Sacagawea would appear on the new dollar coin, we thought the unveiling of the new design was the ideal occasion for an event honoring not just Sacagawea, but the accomplishments of all Native American women.

Right: The Vietnam Era Veterans Inter-Tribal Association Color Guard (VEVITA), Mrs. Clinton, LaDonna Harris, Assistant Secretary for Indian Affairs Kevin Gover, Department of the Treasury Secretary Robert Rubin, and Director of the U.S. Mint Phillip Diehl at the Sacagawea coin ceremony.

Above: Delegates of the
Yanktonai, Santee, Upper
Missouri Lakota, Sac and
Fox, Anishinabe (Ojibwa),
Ottawa, Kickapoo, and
Miami tribes pose with
President Andrew
Johnson on February 23,
1867, at the South Portico.
Their meeting with "The
Great Father"—President
Johnson—was a
ceremonial occasion.

It was a warm spring afternoon in 1999 when the pounding rhythms of the Eyabay drum group reverberated across the South Lawn, welcoming the 750 guests—including representatives from more than 300 tribes—into the pavilion. After a tribal color guard led the speakers to the stage, a prayer was offered by Zelda Tillman, a representative from Sacagawea's Shoshone tribe, and the coin design was unveiled to thunderous applause.

Sacagawea is generally pictured pointing toward the horizon. But for the new coin, a different image was chosen—that of a brave young woman with a child on her back. This rendering, designed by southwestern artist Glenna Goodacre, celebrates not only Sacagawea's courage and strength, but Native American heritage and the accomplishments of women in the earliest days of our history. Tom Rogers of the U.S. Mint designed the flip side of the coin, which features a soaring bald eagle surrounded by 17 stars, representing the number of states at the time of the expedition. I know that when any of our guests from that afternoon—including the many thousands who joined us via cybercast—receives one of these coins in their change they will remember this special day and the coin's special meaning.

Right: Mrs. Clinton joins tribal leaders after the celebration unveiling the Sacagawea coin in 1999.

Left: Joe Martin, a tribal dancer from the Menominee Nation of Wisconsin, at the May 1999 ceremony unveiling the Sacagawea dollar coin issued by the U.S. Mint.

HISTORY IN THE MAKING

Above: Mrs. Clinton at the swearing-in of the first class of AmeriCorps members in September 1994. AmeriCorps members dedicate a year of service to their communities in exchange for education awards. Since 1994, more than 150,000 Americans have served in the program. Opposite page: At the ceremony for the signing of the AmeriCorps bill in September 1993, the President leads enthusiastic volunteers up the South Lawn.

On September 21, 1993, I sat with 1,000 community service activists, business leaders, and others who had come to the South Lawn of the White House to watch the President sign legislation creating AmeriCorps. As the band Soul Asylum played and guests cheered, my husband, surrounded by 100 young people from all over the country, walked over the hill toward a massive pavilion. Some of these young people were mentoring and vaccinating children. Others were cleaning up rivers or building houses for poor families. All were practicing citizen service, just as the President hoped when he first proposed this program to give young people the opportunity to serve their communities and receive help paying for college in return.

The morning of the ceremony, Bill showed me the two very special pens he had used to sign the bill creating AmeriCorps.

Above: Mrs. Clinton and the Reverend Billy Graham at dinner the night before the 1993 National Prayer Breakfast.

One pen had been used by President Franklin Roosevelt to create the Civilian Conservation Corps; the other had been used by President Kennedy to make the Peace Corps a reality. For over 200 years, our country has believed that solving the great problems of the day requires the active participation of its citizens. And for more than 200 years, every President has used the powerful backdrop of the White House to illuminate those challenges.

Below: The First Lady holds a meeting on child care in 1997 with David Hamburg, president of the Carnegie Foundation; First Lady Chief of Staff Melanne Verveer; Domestic Policy Council Staff Nicole Rabner, Jennifer Klein, and Elena Kagan; Health and Human Services Associate Commissioner Joan Lombardi; and Deborah Phillips, National Research Council.

Sometimes late at night, as I walk through the halls of the White House, I think of all the historic issues that have been debated and resolved under this roof, from Thomas Jefferson and Meriwether Lewis planning their expedition across the continent to John F. Kennedy planning to put a man on the moon. My husband and I have tried to use the stature of the White House to draw attention to issues confronting American families today, such as child care, health care, education, youth violence, and gun control. At bill signings, policy announcements, and events designed to illustrate administration positions, we have not only invited government officials and renowned experts, but also the citizens whose lives and families are most directly affected by the President's actions.

The first bill my husband signed into law was the Family and Medical Leave Act of 1993, which has allowed millions of workers to take time off to care for a new child or a seriously ill family member. Even 50 years ago, we never could have predicted the large number of mothers who are

working full-time today. Dozens of them were in the audience for the signing ceremony, grateful that they no longer would have to choose between keeping a job and caring for an infant or sick parent. They were joined by advocates and experts who had championed family leave for many years and who now watched with pride as it became the law of the land.

Even before I moved into the White House, I knew about the work of my predecessors and the causes they had championed. Barbara Bush put the spotlight on literacy. Lady Bird Johnson hosted a conference in the East Room to talk about beautifying America's landscape. Rosalynn Carter held meetings on mental health. Pat Nixon raised awareness about the importance of volunteering, donating time to hospitals, schools, day-care centers, and nursing homes. Nancy Reagan brought together First Ladies from all over the world to talk about drug abuse. Betty Ford talked openly about her struggle with breast cancer, finally bringing this disease out of the shadows.

At the time Mrs. Ford began talking about her personal battle with breast cancer, women all too often suffered the disease in

Above: Anna Wintour, the editor of Vogue, *Princess Diana of Wales, Donald and Katharine Graham of* The Washington Post, *and designer Ralph Lauren join the First Lady to raise public awareness about breast cancer in September 1996. Right: Mrs. Clinton speaks in the East Room, supporting International Women's Day in March 1998.*

Above: The First Lady and Vice President Gore confer the morning of the White House Conference on Child Care in 1997.

silence. But in 1993 it was breast cancer survivors themselves who came to the White House to present Bill and me with a petition calling for a national action plan to wipe out the disease. Since then, we've hosted scientists and activists to advocate for and celebrate unprecedented increases in funding for research, treatment, early detection, and cutting-edge breakthroughs that are saving lives. We showcased a first-of-its-kind breast cancer postage stamp, the proceeds of which are dedicated to research. And we unveiled public service announcements for Mother's Day that encourage older women to get free mammograms under Medicare.

At most of these events, I have remembered and often talked about my mother-in-law, Virginia Kelly, whom we lost to breast cancer in 1994. Even as she battled the disease, she never wanted anyone to feel sorry for her. She got up every day, put on her false eyelashes, and went out to embrace and enjoy life. I remember the sampler she kept next to her bed. It said, "Dear God, there is nothing that can happen today that you and I can't handle." Virginia was a great inspiration to us in life and remains so even now. Whenever we have celebrated advances in the war against breast cancer, we have done so in her memory, and in

the memory of every single mother, sister, daughter, grandmother, colleague, and neighbor whose life has been cut short by this horrible disease.

Over the last 30 years as a lawyer and advocate, I have worked on behalf of the children in our child welfare system and came to the White House determined to improve the lives of children in foster care.

On November 13, 1995, a young girl in foster care in Kansas came to the White House, along with dozens of other foster children, to publicize the plight of children waiting for adoptive families. Dianna moved the entire audience to tears with a poem she had written about her dream. It wasn't to go on a fun vacation or receive a new toy. Dianna's dream was to be adopted. She explained, "The reason I want to be adopted is I would have a place that I could call home. I would have a room that I could call my room. I would have a family that I could love and would love me back." Because of the publicity around her appearance, Dianna's dream came true. Two years later, I invited her back, but this time she came with Sherada and Bill Collins—her new adoptive family.

What we have found through the years is that many parents who want to adopt do

Left: Mrs. Clinton celebrates National Adoption Month with adoptees and their families in November 1998. Below: In 1995, Dianna Collins spoke at the White House about wanting to be adopted. She returned to the White House to celebrate her adoption by Sherada and Bill Collins in 1997.

not know about children like Dianna, who languish in foster care, waiting for permanent homes. For eight years, we used the White House to put a spotlight on all of the children in foster care and increase the number of them who are adopted into safe, loving, permanent homes. For example, when we celebrated National Adoption Day in 1998, we were joined by two well-known former foster care children, Washington, D.C., Mayor Anthony Williams and Dave Thomas, founder of Wendy's restaurants. But the real stars of the afternoon were 24 very special families. One by one, their names

were called in the East Room. One by one, parents proudly stood with their new children. Some were infants, some were teenagers, but all of them a more powerful testament than any statistic or press release every could be.

We have also used the White House to examine important issues in depth and bring cutting-edge information to citizens and policy makers alike. Many of the White House conferences we have held were the first of their kind, including conferences on teenagers, mental health, child care, hate crimes, philanthropy, and early childhood development.

I first studied the issue of early childhood development in law school and knew that brain research now confirmed what parents have always intuitively believed—that the early stimulation a child receives can influence how he or she learns and grows over a lifetime. I wanted more people to know about this research, so I hosted a conference that brought together experts on childhood development, neuroscientists, policy makers, child care providers, community leaders, elected officials, business leaders, teachers, and parents to find ways to give every child a healthy start in life.

One of the biggest problems we always face with such events is how to narrow the guest list down so the participants can fit into the East Room. That's why we started broadcasting these events via satellite to hundreds of locations across the country and, through cybercasting, to the world— a feat that may seem commonplace today, but which was beyond the imagination of even the brilliant founders of our nation 200 years ago.

As much change as we've seen in these two centuries, some things have remained constant. Americans have always looked to the White House to highlight our common challenges and bring us together in good times and bad. When war threatens, citizens turn to hear the President speak directly to them. When tragedy strikes, citizens turn to the White House to express their collective grief and begin to heal together.

Above left: The President and Mrs. Clinton discuss children's issues in the Map Room with entertainer Ricky Martin.
Above right: President Clinton, Bill Cosby, and Linda Ellerbee at the 1996 Conference on Children's Television. Participants discussed ways to improve the quality and quantity of children's programming.

I remember when Bill and I planted white dogwood trees on the east knoll of the South Grounds, one in memory of Commerce Secretary Ron Brown and those who died with him in a plane crash in the Balkans, and one for the men, women, and children murdered in the bombing in Oklahoma City. And I remember how important it was for the President and me to host a meeting to discuss and develop a strategy for a national campaign to address youth violence after the school shootings in Littleton, Colorado, in 1999. Our goal was not only to comfort that community as it mourned, but to use the power of the White House to bring our country together. As my husband has said many times, he could not have predicted when he was sworn in as President how often he would have to lead our nation in mourning and remembrance.

Above: The First Lady meets Brandon Denny, age four, in January 1996. Brandon was injured in the Oklahoma City bombing.
Right: The President and Mrs. Clinton plant a tree on the White House grounds in memory of the victims of the 1995 Oklahoma City bombing.

Every week, thousands of people come by foot, car, train,

bus, subway, and airplane to see their house—the people's

house. The line for the public tour starts forming early in

the morning at the East Visitor's Gate and snakes around the

South Lawn. In line, children wonder whether they will get

a glimpse of Buddy and Socks once they are inside. Senior

citizens, having seen pictures and newscasts their whole

lives, look forward to seeing the White House with their own

eyes. And groups of students and teachers stand ready to see

the history they have studied in the classroom come alive.

It is amazing to imagine that until 1937 there was not even a

fence around the South Lawn. People came and went as they

pleased. Families used this prime spot for their picnics;

children chased each other around the lush grounds. There

are more security restrictions today, but the White House is

still the only residence of a head of state anywhere in the world that is open to the public free of charge.

Most visitors come on the public tours that are available Tuesday through Saturday. They enter through the East Wing and walk to the residence through a glass-enclosed colonnade. From there, they can take a moment to look out over the South Lawn to the Washington Monument, and enjoy one of my favorite places on the grounds—the Sculpture Garden. As they enter the residence on the ground floor, visitors can see the family Library, which contains books about American history and our Presidents; the Vermeil Room, which houses the gold-plated silver pieces (called *vermeil*) that we use for entertaining; and the China Room, designated by Mrs. Woodrow Wilson in 1917 to display the collection of White House china.

Upstairs, on the State Floor, the first stop is the East Room, which many will recognize from news coverage as the site of presidential press conferences, treaty signings, performances, and, on occasion, formal dinners. Here visitors can see the full-length portraits of George and Martha Washington, and imagine the days when President Garfield's children, Irvin and Abram, rode their cycles across the floors. Visitors then walk through the Green Room, the oval-shaped Blue Room, the Red Room, the State Dining Room, the Cross Hall, and the Entrance Hall. And as they leave the building through the North Portico, many pause to take a photograph of their family with the White House as backdrop.

This house and its history belong to all Americans, and we have worked hard to share this national treasure with as many people as possible—not just dignitaries, politicians, or the rich and famous, but Americans from every corner of the country and every walk of life. What follows are just a few examples of the ways we open the doors and invite America in.

White House Easter Egg Roll

From the 10,000 decorated Easter eggs to the 30,000 visitors decked out in their Sunday best, no one does an Easter egg roll quite like the White House—an annual event held on Easter Monday, thanks to hundreds of volunteer "Easter Bunnies." The tradition dates back to at least 1872, when it took place on the

grounds of the United States Capitol. In 1876, though, members of Congress got tired of the rowdy crowds and the remains of hard-boiled eggs scattered everywhere, and they declared that no part of the Capitol grounds would ever be used as a playground again.

Left: Longtime volunteer Bernie Fairbanks hands President Clinton the whistle to officially start the Egg Roll in 1998.

Upon hearing the news, President Rutherford B. Hayes and his wife, Lucy, reassured all forlorn egg rollers that the tradition would continue at the White House. And it has.

Since that time, the Easter Egg Roll has become the largest annual public event on the White House calendar. In fact, its popularity has grown so rapidly that, in 1993, I expanded the site to include the

Opposite page: Striding head and shoulders above the crowd, 1996.

Ellipse so that there would be room for even more activities. In 1998 we featured the first-ever cybercast of the Egg Roll so that children worldwide could join in as well.

On the big day, thousands of parents and children between the ages of three and six wait in line for the gates to open and the festivities to begin. Thousands more gather to watch the spectacle. Some of these children have overcome great obstacles to be at this event. I remember a letter I received about a little girl who attended the Easter Egg Roll in 1999. She is blind, but she told everyone that on that special day she knows she really *saw* the President out on the lawn.

The Easter Egg Roll offers a wonderful opportunity to bring our national history to life for children. When they file in, the children are serenaded by the Marine Band playing Irving Berlin's *Easter Parade* and John Philip Sousa's *Easter Monday on the White House Lawn* and are greeted by the Easter Bunny. Since 1998, professional actors and scholars costumed as historical figures like George Washington, Abigail Adams, and Benjamin Banneker (the grandson of a slave, he was one of the original city surveyors of Washington, D.C.) have joined us, answering the children's questions about our history.

It is sometimes hard to see who is having more fun, the young people or their parents, who often revert back to childhood during these hours. I always make it a point to visit the display of confectionery Easter art, created by talented pastry chefs from around the country. One year I even found a life-sized candy version of Socks climbing out of his own chocolate Easter egg!

The President's favorite moment comes when he gets to blow the ceremonial whistle, signaling the beginning of the Egg Roll. You can see the joy and absolute determination in the faces of the children as they maneuver their oversized plastic spoons to roll, push, or flip brightly colored eggs to the finish line.

I love watching all the children spread out on the lawn enjoying the activities, from storytelling and egg decorating to musical performances and, of course, the big egg hunt. This is no ordinary hunt. In this event, started by Nancy Reagan, some special children have the chance to take home a prized wooden egg autographed by a celebrity or sports figure who has visited the White House during the course of the year.

Left: Children delight in the annual Egg Roll, 1996.

Top: Pastry Chef Roland Mesnier tries his hand at making cotton candy. Middle (from left to right): Elizabeth McGrath, Sandy Wilson, Johnny Wilson, and PHC Charles McGrath (of White House television), strolling the midway during the staff picnic. Bottom: Director of Logistics Laura Schwartz enjoys the picnic festivities.

Picnics

Our family spends a lot of time outside on the White House grounds. Our young nephews, Zachary Rodham and Tyler Clinton, are often found on the swing outside the Oval Office or chasing down golf balls as the President putts them on the South Grounds. Socks, our cat, finds shade under a giant oak tree behind the Oval Office, and Buddy, our dog, enjoys a game of catch on the lawn or a romp in the fountain from time to time.

Throughout our history, these grounds have always been a playground for the President's children, grandchildren, nieces and nephews, and their pets. Benjamin Harrison's grandson Baby McKee was often spotted driving his goat cart, pulled by the famous billy goat His Whiskers. During World War I, Woodrow Wilson's sheep had the run of the South Lawn, as had Teddy Roosevelt's children's pony, Algonquin, and, many years later, Caroline Kennedy's pony, Macaroni.

Eventually, the lawn became a favorite place for entertaining. First Ladies Florence Harding, Nellie Taft, and Eleanor Roosevelt were fond of hosting parties in the lovely gardens. But it was Lyndon Johnson who held the first

White House cookout, a Texas-style barbecue on the West Terrace. Maybe because we're barbecue fans as well, the summer cookout is one of our favorite ways to entertain.

Bill and I have hosted annual picnics for members of Congress, for the White House press corps, and for the White House staff and their families as an acknowledgment of the long hours they spend away from home and the sacrifices they make to serve the public. In addition to the Marine Band, we have featured entertainers such as Trisha Yearwood, David Sanborn, and Kid Creole and the Coconuts. And, thanks to the White House chefs, the food is always one of the highlights of the evening.

As is the case with all social events, the social secretary and I begin planning months ahead, and try to come up with new ideas each year. In 1998 Capricia Marshall and I decided to stage an old-fashioned carnival, complete with a Ferris wheel, daredevil rides, games, cotton candy, and balloon artists for the children.

The carnival was a great hit, but the midsummer heat (which made us wish we had included a dunking booth) persuaded us to schedule the next year's

Please present this card with photo identification at
The Visitor Entrance
The White House

Not Transferable

Top: The carnival midway as seen from a ride
Right and above: The invitation to the carnival

picnics in September. That year we hosted a "Jazz on the Lawn" picnic for members of Congress, where guests got to hear incredible jazz musicians from Chicago and New Orleans. There were servers sporting strands of Mardi Gras beads, and a never-ending spread of catfish fingers, Louisiana crawfish tails, stir-fried alligator, jambalaya, gumbo, pralines, and even Chicago's cheesecake on a stick. Partisan politics were forgotten for a few hours as jazz—the quintessential American art form—worked its magic.

Above: The President and Mrs. Clinton enjoy the entertainment at the press picnic.

Bottom left: Fast food and colorful stuffed animals are all part of the carnival experience.

Below: Director of Special Projects Debby McGinn, Deputy Social Secretary Sharon Kennedy, and Special Assistant for Personal Correspondence Helen Robinson greet guests at the 1998 staff picnic.

Opposite page: White House staffers Roger Salazar and Ginny Terzano sitting on top of the world.

7

DANGER! DO NOT ROCK SEAT

DANGER! DO NOT ROCK SEAT

Above left: Chief Usher Gary Walters and a furry friend; First Assistant Usher Dennis Freemyer is in the background.
Above right: Johnny Muffler worked at the White House as an electrician for fifty years until his death in 1999. His son Rick is a penman in the White House calligraphy office.
Left (from left to right): Ted Danson, Luke Silver-Greenberg, Charlie McDowell, and Mary Steenburgen enjoy a ride.

Right: White House staffer Chris Jennings and his son go for a spin at the staff picnic.
Below left: In line for lunch.
Below right: Chef John Moeller at the grill.

St. Patrick's Day

Traditionally, on St. Patrick's Day, the *taoiseach* (pronounced tee-shock; the prime minister) of Ireland presents a crystal bowl of shamrocks to the President of the United States. In 1994 Ann Stock and I decided to take that simple tradition and turn it into the centerpiece for an annual St. Patrick's Day party. Five years later, the event had grown so much that we moved it to a pavilion on the South Lawn to accommodate the ever-expanding guest list.

Americans have always felt a special kinship with the people of Ireland, because, like my husband, so many trace their family roots there. But the strongest bond between the people who have come to the White House to celebrate St. Patrick's Day during recent years is that they have shared the same dream: peace in Northern Ireland.

The first trip Bill and I took to Belfast was on November 30, 1995. It was the first time a U.S. President had ever visited Northern Ireland. The first cease-fire had just taken place.

That year we wanted our St. Patrick's Day party to be an expression of solidarity with all the peacemakers. In addition to the *taoiseach* of Ireland and other members of the Irish government, we invited representatives of the different parties in the North. Over the years we have also invited a large group of Americans of Irish descent, including celebrities such as Dylan McDermott, Paul Newman, Roma Downey, Michael Keaton, and Aidan Quinn, and featured performances by Irish bagpipers, harpists, pipers, pianists, step-dancers, and choirs. We have heard great Irish vocalists Frank Patterson and Tom Sweeney, listened intently as Frank McCourt read from his Pulitzer prize–winning memoir *Angela's Ashes,* and

Below: The President, the First Lady, and Social Secretary Ann Stock share a lighthearted moment in the Diplomatic Reception Room before the arrival of Prime Minister Bruton of Ireland in March 1996 for a St. Patrick's Day reception. Guests were treated to a magnificent array of Irish favorites, including corned beef and Kerry pies.

Left: Young step-dancers from the O'Neill-James School of Irish Dance stand at attention as the President passes by, March 1998.

Below: Piper Dr. Richard Blair pipes the President and First Lady down the hall to meet their guests in 1998. Dr. Blair played for Presidents Eisenhower and Kennedy and was in charge of the Air Force Pipe Band.

concert pianist who lost her sight in the 1998 Omagh bombing, expressed her dream of peace in a piano tribute she played with Phil Coulter. And it was then that the President awarded the Medal of Freedom to former Senator, international statesman, and son of an Irish immigrant George Mitchell, for the critical role he played in forging the historic Good Friday peace accords.

In accepting his award, Senator Mitchell said, "I have a new dream. In a few years, I will take my young son to Northern Ireland. We will go to the Northern Ireland Assembly, where we will sit quietly in the gallery and watch and listen as these men and women here debate the ordinary issues of life in a democratic society—education, health care, agriculture, tourism. There will be no talk of war, for the war will have long been over. There will be no talk of peace, for peace will be taken for granted. On that day, the day on which peace is taken for granted in Northern Ireland, I will be truly and finally fulfilled."

That night, everyone left the White House inspired to keep working for peace, to ensure that Senator Mitchell's and Claire Gallagher's hopes are realized.

Above: President Clinton presents Senator George Mitchell with the Medal of Freedom in March 1999 for his diplomatic efforts in Northern Ireland.

heard Nobel prize–winning poet Seamus Heaney recite from *The Cure at Troy.* We've also filled up with boxty, corned beef with cabbage roulade, kedgeree cakes, colcannon, Irish cheeses, shortbread, and Irish soda bread, as well as Guinness stout.

Every St. Patrick's Day party leaves us with unforgettable memories, but perhaps the most powerful images I have are from the celebration in 1999. It was there that Claire Gallagher, an aspiring

Above: At the 1998 St. Patrick's celebration, Frank McCourt reads from his Pulitzer prize–winning book Angela's Ashes, *which describes his experiences growing up in poverty in Limerick.*

Right: Massachusetts Senator Ted Kennedy listens attentively to McCourt's reading.

CHRISTMAS AT THE WHITE HOUSE: AN AMERICAN TRADITION

Above: A variety of handcrafted holiday decorations.
Opposite page: In the wee hours of the morning, a crane lifts the enormous wreath that will grace the South Portico.

Not long after my husband's first inauguration, with the after-Christmas sales just winding down, Chief Usher Gary Walters and then Social Secretary Ann Stock sat down with me to deliver some surprising news: It was already time to begin planning for the next Christmas season.

I love Christmas, but I have always been slow to make arrangements, a trait I inherited from my own family. When I was a child, my family followed the old tradition of waiting until Christmas Eve to put up our tree, and we usually did not finish decorating until late that night. My brothers and I baked chocolate chip cookies with our mother while our

Below: The South Portico at night, decorated for the 1998 holiday season.

Above: As tradition dictates, the 1998 White House Christmas tree arrives by horse-drawn wagon to be accepted by the First Lady.
Right: Mrs. Clinton and designer Robert Isabell, with members of his staff, discuss the hanging of the wreath in 1998, the largest ever hung on the White House.

father set up the tree in its stand in our living room. Then we children, often with considerable help from our grandfather, made ornaments out of papier-mâché, tinfoil, pipe cleaners and anything else we could get our hands on.

With only one tree to decorate, we could afford to wait until the last minute. At the White House, however, there are dozens of trees, dozens of parties, and thousands of visitors to prepare for. What I learned in that conversation in 1993 is that I was expected, like the director of a major Broadway show, to oversee all the preparations, from selecting the overall theme of the celebration to the menus, decorations, parties, and music that make it all come alive. Every detail has to be carefully planned and executed with the help of a supporting cast of staff and

volunteers from all over the country. And every detail is intended to make each visitor who walks into the White House—and the millions of others who make a "virtual visit" via the Internet—feel like they are at home.

Every first family adds its unique mark on holiday celebrations at the White House. We have added to those traditions and started some of our own. The children from local schools who take photos with Buddy and Socks and gather around Bill as he reads *'Twas the Night Before Christmas* are following not only a family tradition (since we used to read the same story to Chelsea) but also a 200-year-old White House tradition of filling the house with children during the holidays. Andrew Jackson, whose mother died when he was a small boy, knew the

Above left: At the 1993 press preview, Mrs. Clinton unveils the holiday decorations so that the season's entertaining may begin.
Above right: A 1995 gingerbread replica of Mrs. Clinton's family home in Park Ridge, Illinois.

Above: Director of Special Projects Debby McGinn, Chief Usher Gary Walters, Mrs. Clinton, and Deputy Social Secretary Tracy LaBreque Davis admire the Blue Room Christmas tree, December 1997. The theme for this year was "Santa's Workshop."

Above and left: Volunteers play a significant role in decorating the White House for the holidays. Here they are working on the Blue Room tree in 1998. The chandelier is removed and the tree is anchored from the ceiling. In the photograph on the left are volunteers Tom O'Brien, Sue Streett, Mary Elizabeth Boyd, and Judy Patton.

sadness of a Christmas without toys, friends, and family. As President, he celebrated the holiday by inviting local orphans to a party at the White House, and even joined them for a snowball fight in the East Room complete with "snowballs" made of cotton.

The annual White House Christmas card, sent yearly to 300,000 Americans, was a tradition started by President Eisenhower to convey official holiday greetings to friends, government officials, diplomats, and supporters from around the country. Over the years, we have asked celebrated artists, including Thomas McKnight and Ray Ellis, to depict different parts of the White House as they look during the holiday season. We have featured the Red Room, the Blue Room, the Green Room, the State Dining Room, and winter views of the South and North Porticos warmed by Christmas lights and wreaths.

We've also carried on the tradition begun by Jacqueline Kennedy of decorating the official tree in the Blue Room around one central theme, which we now also use for all the decorations throughout the house. In recent years, the White House has been transformed into such settings as "Santa's Workshop," "Winter Wonderland," and "The Nutcracker Suite," which had

special meaning for us because of the many years we watched Chelsea perform in this holiday favorite. Choosing a theme is the first thing I have to do every year. It is a closely guarded state secret, not revealed to the press and public until the tree and house are fully decorated and the festivities are ready to begin.

There are few events more special at the White House than the arrival of the 18½-foot-high official Christmas tree. The tree travels up the south drive to the door of the White House on a horse-drawn cart, accompanied by members of the family who donated it.

The tradition of a White House Christmas tree was started by Benjamin Harrison in 1889 but almost didn't survive the 19th century. Theodore Roosevelt banned Christmas trees from the house because he believed that chopping down healthy evergreens for the holiday was at odds with his commitment to conservation. Of course, that didn't stop the Roosevelt children from smuggling a small spruce into the attic and keeping it hidden until Christmas. Touched, the President gave in and let the family keep the tree.

During the holiday season, more than 150,000 people of all ages, races, religions,

Opposite page, left: There are Christmas trees in almost every room of the White House. This tree is in the Library on the ground floor.
Opposite page, right: The Family Dining Room, located next to the State Dining Room, where the table is set for the Clinton family's Christmas day dinner.

Above left: The President and Mrs. Clinton in front of the Blue Room tree, 1999.
Above right: The President admires the Blue Room tree in 1995.

Right: President and Mrs. Clinton dance at a 1996 holiday reception while Secretary of Education Richard Riley and Mrs. Riley look on.

*Above: A menu for a
festive holiday dinner*

and ethnicities visit the decorated White House. Some are children with special needs, who come in wheelchairs and braces. Some are older Americans who arrive on buses from as far away as Pennsylvania, Delaware, and New York. Many take special candlelit evening tours, a tradition begun by Mrs. Nixon to enable working people to see the White House decorations.

When guests walk into the Blue Room, they see the White House tree illuminated by 2,700 lights, covered with handmade ornaments, and surrounded by a green velvet tree skirt made for us in 1993 by quilters from every state. I love the

ornaments, which are created every year by volunteers from all over America.

One needlepoint ornament showing a *Nutcracker* scene of a man and woman dancing was created in honor of the artist's late husband, who had been buried at Arlington Cemetery; she wanted her ornament to be as close to him as possible.

One year the tree featured very chic looking Santa and Mrs. Claus ornaments, decked out in fashionable Santa suits made by famous American designers like Oscar de la Renta, Ralph Lauren, and Vera Wang.

I especially liked the ornaments that 20 fifth-graders from Flower Mound, Texas, made out of Styrofoam snowmen, metal stars, and Popsicle sticks. The entire class traveled to Washington to see their handiwork on display—a once-in-a-lifetime experience for the excited artists.

As much as Bill and I love our Christmas traditions, we've wanted to be sure Americans of other faiths felt welcome during the holiday season. In 1993 we put a menorah in the West Wing lobby to honor the Jewish festival of Chanukah. The President also lights another very special menorah in the Oval Office. Maryim Baram, an Israeli craftsman who lost his young son in the 1973 Arab-Israeli War, created it from his love and grief and sent it to the President.

Above: When Marines are at the entrance to the West Wing lobby, the President is in the Oval Office.

Starting in 1996, we have also hosted a Ramadan event to mark the end of the holy month of fasting and prayer for Muslims and to increase understanding of Islam.

When you walk through the house at this time of year, the rooms are filled with the music of schoolchildren, senior citizens, church choir members, pianists, and string musicians, 2,500 of whom are selected each year from around the country to come and perform all over the house during tours and parties.

The mantels in the Red and Green Rooms display scenes created by artists using different media—including, in 1998, decorations made from cake. New York designer Colette Peters created an entire Winter Wonderland scene out of frosted cake, complete with a group of polar bears fishing and a stack of presents piled high.

Most of the artists whose creations appear at the White House are not household names. They come from small towns and big cities, and they represent many different rich traditions of American creativity. By day, they are architecture or culinary students, woodworkers and needle-pointers. For more than thirty years, one artist from the District of Columbia, Lily Spandorf, could be found every holiday season moving from room to room to capture the new decorations with her sketches. Lily died in 1999 and we all miss her.

Visitors may also be greeted by our own version of Santa, played by a U.S. Secret Service Uniformed Division officer.

Above: A drawing
of the Diplomatic
Reception Room
tree, 1993, by Lily
Spandorf.

Right: Mrs. Clinton greets
a young visitor on a special
holiday tour for people
with disabilities, 1993.
Below: The President
and Mrs. Clinton read
'Twas the Night Before
Christmas, a White House
tradition.

He even has an official White House I.D. reading "Santa."

As in any home during the holidays, the air of the White House is filled with the smell of those irresistible sweets that we eat every December and, too often, regret every January. White House guests may sample one of 100,000 or so cookies and pastries, or a slice of one of 250 fruitcakes that have been marinating in our walk-in refrigerators since July. They are all made by White House Pastry Chef Roland Mesnier and his assistants. Roland's holiday baking uses approximately 500 pounds of sugar and 300 pounds of chocolate!

Roland surprises us every year with one of his trademark gingerbread houses, which is always elaborate and 100 percent edible. He has fashioned Bill's childhood home in Hope, Arkansas; Santa's workshop at the North Pole, complete with a modern Santa holding a cell phone to check out the weather conditions for flying; and, one year, a fairyland castle guarded by marzipan figures of Buddy and Socks on skates.

Some of the liveliest Christmas moments, however, happen behind the scenes during the three days in early December when the White House closes its doors to be decorated.

The "elves" who undertake the daunting task of transforming the White House into a magical wonderland are volunteers, mostly professional florists and decorators from all over the country. In 1998 they were joined by Robert Isabell, an orchestrater of wonderful events whose creative team worked with Social Secretary Capricia Marshall, Chief Usher Gary Walters, and Floral Designer Nancy Clarke to plan and execute the decorations—including, for the first time, a giant wreath hung on the Truman Balcony.

The volunteers love the house and return year after year, some for 15, 20, and, in one case, 27 years. In fact, the chief floral designer of the White House, Nancy Clarke, started as a volunteer herself more than 20 years ago. When they come together for the long weekend, it is almost like a family reunion, only this one is spent putting up the ornaments; hanging more than 300 wreaths; stringing 720 lengths of garland on mantels, windows, and doorways; setting up the plants and flowers; and otherwise getting the house ready for Christmas.

Above: The White House crèche was redesigned in 1999 to resemble the style of traditional Italian crèches.

Right: A volunteer puts the finishing touches on a holiday wreath hung from the ceiling in the East Room. Below left: Another volunteer adjusts a golden tree in the East Room. Below right: The President and members of the Social Office staff in a holiday moment in the Diplomatic Reception Room (from left to right): Robyn Dickey, Tracy LaBrecque Davis, Sarah Farnsworth Burke, President Clinton, Capricia Marshall, Ann Stock.

THE WHITE HOUSE, *The Green Room, 1996*

THE WHITE HOUSE, *The State Dining Room, 1998*

Above left: The 1997 Christmas card featured Kay Jackson's rendition of the White House at night. The view depicted is from the South Lawn.

Above right: The 1996 Christmas card featured a painting of the Green Room by Thomas McKnight. The painting is one of a series produced by the artist, which also included the Red Room in 1994 and the Blue Room in 1995.

Left: The 1998 Christmas card featured artist Ray Ellis's rendition of the refurbished State Dining Room. He also painted the North Portico for the 1999 Christmas card.

We love watching this transformation, and find time to drop by unannounced to visit with volunteers. Sometimes we even tip-toe downstairs late at night to sneak a peak when everyone has gone home.

And every year, after the official parties have ended several days before Christmas, we begin our own private celebration.

Some things have changed in recent years—like the joy of having young nephews around and the excitement of having our daughter home from college. But most of our traditions—passed down from our own parents or started during our first holidays together as a family—remain the same. The President joins other last-minute shoppers at local stores

Above left: Mrs. Clinton surprises senior citizens on a holiday tour of the White House, December 1993. Above right: On the first night of Chanukah, the President plays a traditional game of dreidel with local children.

Above: Traditionally, the Clintons host holiday dinners in many rooms of the White House. Here, the Diplomatic Reception Room is the venue for 1996 festivities.

Below: Mrs. Clinton enjoys conversation with a guest at a 1999 holiday dinner in the Red Room.

Right: Master needlepoint artist, Hyla Hurley of Washington, D.C., created this "Santa in His Sleigh" kissing ball, which was displayed in the Grand Foyer during the 1997 holiday season.

on Christmas Eve. We still bake cookies and sing carols. And every year, we unpack all of our ornaments and colored lights, and, as Bill stands on a ladder hanging them on our tree in the upstairs Yellow Oval Room, we retell the story and meaning behind each one.

We have dinner together on Christmas Eve with family and friends before attending church services at the National Cathedral. On Christmas morning, after we open gifts and eat too much, our home looks a lot like many others. All that is left of Christmas are our memories and gifts, scraps of wrapping paper and bows, the laughter and excitement of family members, and our gratitude for the spirit of the season.

Above: The President opens his presents on Christmas morning, 1995.

Left: Chelsea and her parents share a private moment before a holiday party, 1995.

Right: The mantel in the Yellow Oval Room, hung with the Clinton family's Christmas stockings.

Far right: The President, his mother, Virginia Kelly, and his brother, Roger Clinton, during Virginia's last Christmas, 1993.

Left: The Clintons and the Gores exchange Christmas gifts in the Center Hall, 1997.

Right: The President and his brother film each other on Christmas morning.

Above: Chelsea and Zachary Rodham admire the family Christmas tree.

Right: Tyler Clinton reviews the Christmas decor, 1995.

CELEBRATING THE MILLENNIUM

Above: Mrs. Clinton, Washington, D.C., Mayor Anthony Williams, and Robert DeNiro in conversation at dinner. Opposite page: The Jacqueline Kennedy Garden was transformed into a glittering jazz club. The sculptures on the left are entitled Willy, Argus, and Lucky *(1996–97), by Deborah Butterfield.*

As I write this, I know our family will soon be packing up and getting ready to leave the house we've called home these past eight years. We're taking with us far more than we brought to the White House that first day in January 1993. I'm not referring to personal belongings, but rather to memories, friendships, and experiences.

While selecting the photos for this book, I saw again the faces of people from all walks of life whom Bill and I welcomed to the White House, from South African President Nelson Mandela and Princess Diana to Special Olympian Sophia Wesolowsky and former foster child Dianna Collins.

I was reminded of others with whom I have spent time here. Some were leaders, such as Jim Brady and Rosa Parks, whose personal courage helped to spark national movements. Others were pioneers in their field, such as

Top: Technicians assemble two blown-glass trees by glass artist Dale Chihuly.
Bottom: A tree welcomes guests in the Grand Foyer.

astronaut Eileen Collins, the first woman to command the space shuttle, and Dr. Francis Collins, who is directing the Human Genome Project at the National Institutes of Health. And many were ordinary Americans who had accomplished extraordinary things, such as Mat Dawson, Jr., a 79-year-old forklift operator who gave to charity over $1 million he made by working overtime, and Hector and Susan Badeau, who, after adopting 22 children, also opened their home to a family of eight from Kosovo.

For us, the White House has been the setting for some of the most important milestones of the past decade: the place where the President and his advisers mapped out the strategy for NATO's intervention in Kosovo, where they worked for peace in Northern Ireland, and where we witnessed the signing of historic legislation to balance the budget and decrease crime.

And it has also been our family's home.

So, while I will miss the extraordinary history of the house—its rooms, portraits, and furnishings—I will also miss the personal moments we shared here: playing in the snow with Buddy on the South Lawn and watching football games in our little kitchen upstairs with the residence staff. Seeing the fireworks from the roof on the Fourth of July and playing catch with Bill in the Rose Garden as we both prepared to throw out first pitches on opening day. I will miss the sun streaming onto the Truman Balcony in the morning and setting through the fan-shaped window in the West Sitting Hall.

Above left: The President welcomes Sophia Loren. Above right: Jack Nicholson and the President.

Above left: The Rose Garden was turned into a disco for New Year's Eve.

Above right: The President, Mrs. Clinton, and Chelsea at the Lincoln Memorial.

Right: Mary Wilson, formerly of the Supremes, sings in the New Year.

Over the last eight years, this house has also seen many of life's changes, both good and bad. We lost Bill's mother and my father and close friends such as Ron Brown and Vince Foster. We weathered investigations and impeachment. But we also watched our daughter grow from a teenager into a young woman. We welcomed two new nephews to the family and saw young staff members blossom into seasoned professionals, husbands, wives, and parents. And we marked a new century and millennium.

I read about how our predecessors celebrated the New Year, starting with John and Abigail Adams who opened the White House to the public for the first time on New Year's day in 1801. This tradition became so popular that by January 1, 1901, a line four-people deep started forming at dawn. That day, President McKinley ended up shaking hands with more than 5,000 guests.

To prepare for the new millennium, we wanted to use the White House to honor America's past and imagine its future—and to throw one of the best New Year's Eve parties ever.

Above: The President and Chelsea celebrate with a dance, New Year's Eve, 1999.

Above: Will Smith, Mohammed Ali, and Quincy Jones in the East Room.

In the days after Christmas we took down the trees and ornaments and started decorating for the big event. Artist Dale Chihuly built glass trees piece by piece in the Entrance Hall. The flower shop put together festive arrangements of white orchids, greenery, and silver ornaments. The White House chefs began preparing the meal for the millennium evening, including beluga caviar, lobster, and truffle-marinated rack of lamb. And to expand the boundaries of the house, we constructed tents over the Rose Garden and the Sculpture Garden.

When December 31 finally arrived the house glowed with white lights and decorations. We began the evening with a dinner in the East Room in honor of some of America's greatest creators and innovators. And to make it a family affair, we invited the children of our guests to dine in the Rose Garden.

At tables shimmering with white china sat some of the people who shaped this century—from Mohammed Ali to Dave Brubeck, and from Arthur Schlesinger to Sophia Loren, who had been rescued by American troops in Italy during World War II. A few days after the event Loren wrote this to us, "1940, Naples Italy: a little girl starving and terrified by the air bombings. And now, year 2000, at the opening of the third millennium, the same girl sitting at the side of President Bill Clinton, at the White House. Who says Cinderella's fairy tale can't come true?"

After dinner, we all bundled up and joined hundreds of thousands of Americans at the Lincoln Memorial for the gala put together by Quincy Jones and George Stevens, Jr. The mall reverberated with the songs and words of Will Smith, Kenny Rogers, Kathy Mattea, Bono, Trisha Yearwood, Sam Waterston, Don McLean, Tom Jones, and Luther Vandross.

As we moved closer to twelve o'clock, a film, *The Unfinished Journey,* by Steven Spielberg, with original music by John Williams, highlighted some of the pivotal moments of the last hundred years. Shortly before midnight, my husband closed the century by urging us all to embrace "our shared humanity," and then, with only seconds to go, five children lit a fuse, which ran along the reflecting pool and illuminated the entire Washington Monument at the exact stroke of midnight.

But the celebration was far from over. We invited a thousand guests to come back to the White House with us. All night, people danced in the East Room to music by former Supreme Mary Wilson. They celebrated in the Sculpture Garden, which became a jazz club for the evening, and in the Rose Garden, which had been transformed into a disco for the occasion. In the morning we greeted the artists, scholars, scientists, and sports heroes who gave workshops all weekend long at the Smithsonian museums as part of America's Millennium celebration.

In my husband's New Year's Eve toast, he had said, "Tonight we rise to the mountaintop of a new millennium. Behind us we see a great expanse of the American experience, and before us, vast frontiers of possibility still to be explored."

In many ways, that is the challenge that has faced every first family who has lived in this remarkable house—how to honor what lies behind us and how to prepare for what may be ahead.

Even after living here eight years, I still look at the White House with the same awe I felt as a little girl pressing my face up to the gate to get a better look. I sometimes walk down to the Children's Garden on the South Lawn. There, in a shaded spot, is a pond with small

Above: The performance troop Stomp performs at America's Millennium on the steps of the Lincoln Memorial.

handprints around it. These prints were made by grandchildren of the first families who have lived in the White House. We have all left our handprints here, in a way, in the history we have preserved and passed on and the new chapters we have written.

It was the greatest privilege of my life to spend the last eight years at the White House—at home with history.

Recipes

FROM THE

White House

Kitchens

~

DINING AT THE WHITE HOUSE

Dining at the White House may be a simple breakfast tray for a guest, a quiet dinner for the first family, or a State Dinner for 220. It may be coffee with a visiting head of state after an arrival ceremony, a luncheon for governors' spouses in the Yellow Oval Room in the residence, a reception in the State Dining Room, or a dessert buffet in a pavilion on the South Lawn. Whatever the occasion, Executive Chef Walter Scheib, Pastry Chef Roland Mesnier, and their staffs are up to the challenge, even when dinner for two turns into a buffet supper for 30.

When I hired Chef Scheib, I asked him to make the food at the White House as good as that served in the best American restaurants. His recipes take their inspiration from regional American cuisine, and take advantage of the unprecedented variety of produce and products available year-round. The new White

Inset, page 214: Cups and saucers from the Truman state china service
On pages 214 and 215: Executive Chef Walter Scheib puts the finishing touches on a tray of appetizers while Assistant Chef Keith Luce and part-time chef Heiko Meisel observe.
Left: A salt cellar and a spoon inscribed PRESIDENT'S HOUSE *rest on a silver tray.*

House cuisine showcases the best and freshest ingredients, combined in unusual and exciting ways, enhanced with light sauces, not overpowered by butter and cream. It is food that is lower in fat without sacrificing flavor.

Dessert, of course, is always a time to indulge a little. At the White House, Pastry Chef Mesnier may choose to dazzle dinner guests with a stunning display of spun sugar art accompanying a decadently rich cake, or present a tray of delicate cookies for a more informal reception.

In this section you'll find a selection of recipes from the White House kitchens, including Maple-Almond French Toast with Maple-Ginger Pears; Poached Lobster with Marinated Orange Salad, Saffron-Scented Basmati Rice, and Emerald Cilantro Chutney; and Strawberries and Lemon Cream in Chocolate Baskets. All the recipes have been served at White House events, and adapted for the home kitchen. Because White House guests are served American style, with their entrée,

side dishes, and sauces already arranged artfully on a plate, a recipe may have several components. Consider each one separately, and don't be afraid to try only one part of a dish if another part of the recipe isn't appealing or the ingredients aren't readily available.

The photographs, too, show the dishes presented as they would be if they were served at the White House. If it's easier for you to serve your entrée family style, the food will still taste delicious. In the case of the Strawberries and Lemon Cream and the Autumn Bounty, the recipes give specific instructions on making individual servings, since most home cooks won't have the proper equipment to prepare the dessert as Pastry Chef Mesnier does.

Over the past eight years, our guests and family members have found the food at the White House to be elegant, healthful, and delicious. It is the cuisine for the new millennium. So, from the White House to your house, we hope you enjoy it. Bon appétit!

$\mathscr{B}$REAKFAST AND BRUNCH DISHES

Herbed Tomato Frittata with Chicken Chorizo,
Yukon Gold Hash Browns, and Tomato Compote

Maple-Almond French Toast with Maple-Ginger Pears

herbed tomato frittata
with chicken chorizo,
yukon gold hash browns,
and tomato compote

FOR THE TOMATO COMPOTE

10 large plum tomatoes
1½ tablespoons balsamic vinegar
1½ tablespoons extra-virgin olive oil
1 teaspoon fines herbes (see note)
salt, freshly ground black pepper

A sophisticated variation on the traditional American breakfast of eggs, sausage, and potatoes, this is perfect for a leisurely Sunday brunch. The White House kitchens make their own sausage; your favorite commercial brand will do just fine.

NOTE

Fines herbes are a mixture of finely chopped chervil, chives, parsley, and tarragon.

SERVES 8

TOMATO COMPOTE

YIELD: 2½ CUPS

The tomato compote can be prepared 2 days in advance and stored in the refrigerator in an airtight container.

Preheat oven to 200 degrees Fahrenheit.

Line a jelly roll pan with foil and place a wire rack in pan. Cut the tomatoes in half and place on the rack, cut side up.

In a small bowl combine the vinegar and olive oil and drizzle over the tomatoes. Sprinkle with *fines herbes,* salt, and freshly ground black pepper. Place tomatoes in the oven for 4–5 hours or until they are slightly dry and firm. Allow the tomatoes to cool to room temperature. Peel the tomatoes and chop them coarsely. Reserve 1 cup of the tomato compote for the frittata and use the remaining compote as garnish.

FOR THE CHORIZO

1 tablespoon plus 2 teaspoons olive oil

½ cup minced onions

½ cup minced shallots

2 teaspoons minced garlic

1 teaspoon hot paprika

1 teaspoon salt

16 ounces ground chicken

4 ounces minced pancetta

1 tablespoon sugar

1 tablespoon chopped parsley

1 tablespoon chopped chives

1 tablespoon chopped oregano

½ teaspoon fennel seed

¼ teaspoon crushed red pepper

¼ teaspoon black pepper

4–5 feet sausage casings (see note)

⁓ **NOTE**

You may use purchased sausages instead. Sausage casings can be purchased from a local butcher shop.

CHICKEN CHORIZO

*Y*IELD: 8 LINKS

The chorizo can be made 1 day in advance.

Heat 2 teaspoons olive oil in a small sauté pan for 1 minute over low heat. Add the onions and cook for 4–5 minutes or until translucent, stirring occasionally. Add the shallots and cook for 2–3 minutes, stirring frequently. Add the garlic and cook for 1 minute. Add the paprika and ½ teaspoon salt. Mix the ingredients well and cook for 30 seconds. Allow the onion mixture to cool to room temperature.

In a large bowl combine the cooled onion mixture with the chicken, pancetta, remaining salt, sugar, and herbs. Use a wooden spoon to mix well. Chill the sausage mixture while preparing the casing.

Soak the casing in cold water for 15 minutes. Rinse and allow water to run through the inside of the casing.

Fit a large pastry bag with a #10 plain tip and then fill with the sausage mixture, making sure there are no air pockets in the meat. Twist the end of the pastry bag to keep sausage mixture in place.

Tie a knot at one end of the casing. Wet the piping tip and carefully thread on the open end of casing. Slowly squeeze the sausage mixture into the casing, taking care not to overstuff. The sausage will form a coil as it is filled. Leave the end of the casing open while forming links.

To form links: Starting at the knotted end of the casing, twist the sausage into 6-inch-long links and tie off each end with fine twine. Reverse the direction as you twist the next link. If the casing becomes too tight with sausage mixture, squeeze the mixture toward the open end of the casing. Leave the sausages in a rope, cover with plastic wrap, and chill for a minimum of 2 hours or overnight.

(continues)

herbed tomato frittata, *continued*

When ready to cook the chorizo, pierce each sausage 3–4 times with the tip of a sharp knife. Brush the sausages lightly with oil and place in a large nonstick sauté pan over medium heat. Cook the chorizo, turning several times, for 10–12 minutes or until the juices run clear when the sausage is pierced with a sharp knife. The chorizo should be nicely browned. Serve warm.

YUKON GOLD HASH BROWNS

Place the potatoes in a medium-size pot, cover with cold water, and add ½ teaspoon salt. Bring the potatoes to a boil over medium heat and cook for 12–15 minutes. Remove the potatoes from the water and allow to cool to room temperature. Peel the potatoes and grate on the coarse side of a box grater. Place the grated potatoes in a medium-size bowl, add the chives, salt and pepper, and mix well. Form the mixture into 8 pancakes.

Heat a large nonstick sauté pan over medium-high heat for 2–3 minutes. Add 2 tablespoons butter and swirl to coat the bottom of the pan. Place the pancakes into the pan and cook for 4–5 minutes on each side. Using a spatula, move the pancakes and add additional butter so they brown evenly. Keep warm until ready to serve.

FRITTATA

Place the diced potatoes in a medium-size pot, cover with cold water, and add ¼ teaspoon salt. Bring the potatoes to a boil over medium heat, then reduce heat to low and simmer for 12–15 minutes. Drain the potatoes and place in a medium-size bowl with 1 tablespoon clarified butter, tossing to coat.

Wash the minced leeks in standing water to get rid of any sand or grit. Lift the leeks out of the water and drain in a colander.

Heat ¼ cup clarified butter in a large nonstick skillet for 1–2 minutes. Add the onions and cook for 4–5 minutes or until translucent. Add the drained leeks,

FOR THE HASH BROWNS

2 large Yukon Gold potatoes
salt, freshly ground black pepper
½ cup chopped chives
4 tablespoons softened butter

FOR THE FRITTATA

2 cups ½-inch diced, peeled Yukon Gold
  potatoes
salt, freshly ground black pepper
¾ cup clarified butter
½ cup minced wild leeks or leeks, root
  end trimmed
½ cup minced onion
2 tablespoons minced shallots
1 tablespoon minced garlic
1 cup tomato compote
1 cup chopped chervil
16 eggs
½ cup heavy cream

the shallots, and the garlic and cook for 2–3 minutes or until the leeks are wilted. Add the tomato compote, blanched potatoes, and chervil and mix well. Remove the vegetable mixture from heat and place in a large bowl. Wash out the sauté pan so it may be used to cook the frittata. Allow the vegetable mixture to cool for 10–15 minutes, stirring occasionally.

Preheat oven to 350 degrees Fahrenheit. Beat the eggs and cream together in a large bowl. Add 1 teaspoon salt and ½ teaspoon freshly ground black pepper and whisk to blend. Add the egg mixture to the cooled vegetables and mix well.

Heat sauté pan over high heat for 2–3 minutes, add the remaining scant ½ cup clarified butter, and heat for 1 minute. Mix the eggs and vegetables and carefully pour into the hot butter. Reduce the heat to low and cook for 3–4 minutes. Place the sauté pan in a preheated oven and bake for 15–18 minutes or until eggs are set. Using a rubber spatula, loosen the cooked frittata and turn it out onto a warm platter.

TO SERVE

Cut the frittata into wedges and serve with chicken chorizo, Yukon Gold hash browns, and tomato compote.

A rich almond—cream cheese filling sandwiched between crisp batter-dipped slices of toast is a delicious surprise. In this picture, an individual serving is shown on the Truman china.

maple-almond french toast
with maple-ginger pears

ERVES 8

FOR THE PEARS

1 tablespoon lemon juice

2 tablespoons chopped crystallized
   ginger

½ cup water

½ cup packed, light brown sugar

1 large, firm pear or 8 ounces dried
   pear, diced

½ cup maple syrup

½ cup toasted almond slivers

FOR THE FILLING

⅓ cup cream cheese, room temperature

2½ tablespoons almond paste

1 tablespoon maple syrup

1 teaspoon lemon juice

1 teaspoon lemon zest

1 tablespoon packed, light brown sugar

FOR THE TOAST BATTER

6 large eggs

¾ cup heavy cream

1 teaspoon vanilla

2 teaspoons almond extract

¼ teaspoon cinnamon

3 tablespoons honey

2 (8-inch) loaves of bread, about
   1 pound each (see note)

1 tablespoon butter

NOTE

Homemade white bread, brioche, or
Sally Lunn works well with this
recipe.

MAPLE-GINGER PEARS

YIELD: 2 CUPS

The Maple-Ginger Pears can be made ahead and stored in the refrigerator in an airtight container. Warm gently over medium heat before serving.

In a medium-size saucepan combine the lemon juice, crystallized ginger, water, and brown sugar. Bring to a boil and cook for 3–4 minutes over high heat. Add the diced pear, bring back to a boil, and cook for 5–6 minutes over high heat. Mixture will be at a rolling boil, with large bubbles. Add the maple syrup, allow the mixture to return to a boil, and continue cooking 1 minute. Remove from heat, add toasted almonds, and serve warm.

MAPLE-ALMOND FILLING

YIELD: ⅔ CUP

The Maple-Almond Filling may be made 1 day ahead.

In a small bowl cream together the cream cheese and almond paste, using the back of a fork. Add the maple syrup and continue mixing to break up any remaining lumps. Add the lemon juice, lemon zest, and brown sugar. Whip the mixture until creamy and well combined. Cover and store in refrigerator until ready to assemble French toast.

TOAST BATTER

YIELD: 2⅓ CUPS BATTER

Batter may be prepared the night before and stored in the refrigerator in an airtight container.

(continues)

Whisk the eggs to combine, then add the cream, vanilla, and almond extract. Mix in the cinnamon and honey and pour the batter into an 8 x 8 x 2-inch baking dish.

Cover and store in refrigerator until ready to prepare French toast.

TO MAKE FRENCH TOAST

Cut bread into 16 ¾-inch-thick slices. Spread 8 slices of bread with 1 tablespoon Maple-Almond Filling and cover with a slice of bread to form a sandwich. Cut away crusts if desired.

Dip 2 sandwiches into the batter. Let the batter soak in, then turn the sandwiches over, repeating the process; remove the sandwiches to a tray lined with waxed paper. Repeat with remaining sandwiches. Once all the sandwiches are on the tray, spoon any remaining batter over the top, turn the sandwiches over, and repeat. Allow to stand for 2–3 minutes to absorb all the batter.

Preheat oven to 225 degrees Fahrenheit and place a tray lined with foil on the center rack.

Heat a medium-size sauté pan over medium heat for 2 minutes. Add 1 teaspoon butter and allow the butter to foam. Add 2 sandwiches and cook for 2 minutes on each side or until golden brown and cooked through. Remove cooked toast to warm oven. Add ½ teaspoon butter to sauté pan for each additional batch of toast, placing cooked toast in warm oven.

TO SERVE

Cut each French toast sandwich in half, on the diagonal. Arrange each serving of toast on a warm plate with some warmed Maple-Ginger Pears. Garnish the toast with confectioners' sugar, candied lemon zest, toasted almond slivers, and fresh fruit as desired. Serve with soft butter on the side.

FIRST COURSES/HORS D'OEUVRES

Spinach and Roasted Pepper Rolls with Goat Cheese

D'Anjou Pear, Sun-Dried Cranberries, and Stilton Cheese
in a Walnut Tart Shell

Smoked Salmon on Potato Pancakes with
Wheat Berry Caviar and Chive Cream

New Potatoes with Lobster and Bacon

Caramel Pork with Raisin Dressing Baked in Crust

Cajun Seared Scallops with Root Vegetable Slaw
and Old Bay Biscuits

spinach and roasted pepper rolls
with goat cheese

2 tablespoons olive oil
¼ cup minced onions
1½ teaspoons minced garlic
8 ounces crumbled, fresh goat cheese
salt, freshly ground black pepper
1 pound fresh spinach, stemmed
2 red bell peppers
4 sheets phyllo dough, 12 × 18 inches

*Y*IELD: 16 PIECES

Heat 1 teaspoon olive oil in a small skillet over medium-low heat, add onions, and cook, stirring occasionally, for 5–6 minutes or until translucent. Add the garlic and cook for an additional minute. Remove the onions and garlic from heat and cool to room temperature. In a medium-size bowl mix the goat cheese, onions, and garlic. Season with salt and freshly ground black pepper.

Wash the spinach several times to remove sand and grit. Lift out of standing water. Place wet spinach leaves in a large pot with a tight-fitting lid. Season spinach with salt, cover, and cook over high heat 1 minute; stir once and cook for an additional 1–2 minutes or until spinach wilts. Place spinach in ice water to stop the cooking and retain the bright green color, then remove to a colander to drain.

*T*hese savory morsels are a welcome addition to a plate of hors d'oeuvres before dinner.

Roast the peppers over an open flame or under a broiler until skins are charred. Place the roasted peppers in a paper bag to steam for 10 minutes. Peel peppers and cut into ¼-inch strips.

TO ASSEMBLE ROLL

Preheat oven to 375 degrees Fahrenheit. Lay out phyllo dough and cover with plastic wrap and a damp towel to prevent dough from drying out. Brush 1 sheet of phyllo dough with olive oil, then layer with remaining sheets of phyllo dough, brushing each layer with olive oil.

Squeeze any remaining water from spinach and chop coarsely. Start at the long end of the phyllo dough sheet and spread spinach over the bottom third, leaving a 1-inch border at the bottom and sides. Place strips of pepper horizontally, in an even layer, over spinach. Carefully spread a layer of goat cheese mixture over the peppers. Fold in the 1-inch borders at the short ends of the roll to prevent the filling from leaking. Working from the side closest to you, carefully roll phyllo around filling while tucking in sides as you go. Place the roll, seam-side down, on a baking sheet. Brush the top and sides with olive oil and bake in oven for 15–20 minutes or until golden brown. Cool roll for about 30–40 minutes and then cut into 16 slices about 1⅛ inches in width.

FOR THE CRUST

⅓ cup toasted walnuts

1¾ cups flour

¼ teaspoon salt

¼ pound cold unsalted butter,
*   cut into ½-inch pieces*

1 whole egg

1 egg yolk

3 tablespoons cold water

d'anjou pear, sun-dried cranberries, and stilton cheese
in a walnut tart shell

ERVES: 16—18

TO MAKE DOUGH

In the work bowl of a food processor fitted with metal blade, pulse walnuts until finely ground. Remove the ground nuts to a large bowl. Combine the flour and salt in the work bowl and pulse a few seconds. Add the butter and pulse until the mixture resembles coarse crumbs. Add the flour and butter mixture to the ground nuts and mix well with a wooden spoon.

In a small bowl combine the egg, egg yolk, and water and mix well. In a stream, slowly pour the egg mixture into the flour mixture, stirring continuously until the dough forms a ball. Flatten the ball into a disk, cover with plastic wrap, and chill for 2 hours or overnight.

TO MAKE TART SHELL

Roll out dough to a 14-inch circle; the dough should be about ⅛ inch thick. Fit the dough in a 10 or 11 x 1-inch tart pan with a removable bottom. Trim the dough so about ½ inch overhangs the pan. Fold the dough over and press against the inside of pan to reinforce the edge. Prick the dough with the tines of a fork every inch or so. Chill the tart shell for 20–30 minutes.

Preheat oven to 375 degrees Fahrenheit. Line the tart shell with aluminum foil and fill with pie weights or dried beans. Place the tart shell on a sheet pan and bake for 15–20 minutes or until the dough is set.

To finish baking tart shell, remove the foil and pie weights or dried beans and continue baking the tart shell for an additional 5 minutes or until light brown.

(continues)

Deeply flavored

Stilton cheese combines

with buttery pears and

tart cranberries in this

rich and savory tart.

It can be served as an

appetizer or accompanied

by a lightly dressed green

salad after an entrée.

These tarts are displayed

on silver trays and a lace

tablecloth from the White

House collection.

FOR THE FILLING

1 cup sun-dried cranberries

⅓ cup port wine

½ pound Stilton cheese, crumbled

1⅓ cups toasted walnuts, chopped

1 cup heavy cream

2 eggs

2 egg yolks

½ teaspoon minced garlic

salt, freshly ground black pepper

2 peeled, cored, and sliced D'Anjou pears

Remove the tart shell from the oven and cool to room temperature before filling. Reduce oven to 325 degrees Fahrenheit.

Combine the cranberries and port wine in a glass measure. Microwave the cranberries on high for 30 seconds, then allow them to cool to room temperature and absorb the port wine.

TO ASSEMBLE

Fill the baked tart shell with even layers of crumbled Stilton cheese, walnuts, and cranberries. In a medium-size bowl whisk the cream, eggs, and egg yolks until smooth. Add the garlic, salt, and freshly ground black pepper and mix well. Slowly pour the custard into the prepared tart shell. Arrange the pear slices, in a decorative pattern, on top of the filled tart shell. Bake the tart for 40–45 minutes or until golden brown and the filling is set. Place the tart on a cooling rack, and after 5 minutes remove the ring. Allow the tart to cool until slightly warm. Use a large spatula to move tart to a serving plate, then slice and serve immediately.

An elegant

combination of

flavors with an

unexpected twist.

FOR THE SALMON ROSETTES

8 ounces presliced, smoked salmon

FOR THE WHEAT BERRY CAVIAR

1 cup cooked wheat berries (see note)
½ teaspoon squid ink (see note)
pinch salt

FOR THE CHIVE CREAM

2 tablespoons chopped chives (see note)
¼ cup crème fraîche (see note)
2 teaspoons lemon juice
pinch salt, freshly ground black pepper

~ NOTES

Wheat berries are available in health food stores. One-half cup uncooked wheat berries, cooked in 2 cups of water for 1 hour, will yield just over 1 cup cooked wheat berries.

Squid ink can be purchased from a good local fishmonger and is sold by the half ounce.

Purchase 2 bunches of chives to have enough for both the Chive Cream and potato pancakes. Extra chives can be used for garnish.

Crème fraîche, a tangy-tasting, thickened cream, is a specialty of France. French and American versions can be purchased in gourmet markets.

smoked salmon on potato pancakes
with wheat berry caviar and chive cream

𝒴IELD: 16 SALMON ROSETTES

ON POTATO PANCAKES WITH GARNISH

SMOKED SALMON ROSETTES

Cut salmon slices in half lengthwise so each strip is about 1½ inches wide. Start with the narrow end of each strip and roll it up, keeping the cut end neat. This will be the bottom side of the rosette and will help keep the rosette from falling over. Place rosette cut end down on a tray lined with waxed paper. Using a fingertip, push open the edges of the salmon to resemble a rose. Repeat process to make 16 rosettes. Cover and store in refrigerator.

WHEAT BERRY CAVIAR

The Wheat Berry Caviar may be prepared 1 day in advance and stored in the refrigerator in an airtight container.

In a medium-size bowl combine the warm, cooked wheat berries with ½ teaspoon of squid ink. The squid ink will be in a small clump. Toss and mix the berries so the squid ink disperses and thoroughly coats the wheat berries. Cover and allow the warm berries to absorb the squid ink. After the mixture has cooled, taste and season with salt. Cover and store in the refrigerator until ready to assemble the salmon and the potato pancakes.

CHIVE CREAM

Chive Cream may be prepared 1 day in advance and stored in the refrigerator in an airtight container.

In a small bowl combine the chopped chives, crème fraîche, and lemon juice. Stir the Chive Cream until well combined and season with just a pinch of salt

(continues)

and freshly ground black pepper. Cover and store in the refrigerator until ready to assemble the salmon and the potato pancakes.

POTATO PANCAKES

Yield: 16 (2- to 2½-inch) pancakes

Heat 1 tablespoon clarified butter in a medium-size sauté pan, over medium heat, for 1 minute. Add the onion and cook 3–4 minutes or until translucent. Remove the onion to a bowl to cool and wipe out the pan. In a medium-size bowl add the grated potato, lemon juice, flour, and egg. Using a fork, toss the ingredients together until the egg is well mixed. Add the chives, garlic, cooled onion, and salt and toss gently until all ingredients are well combined.

Preheat oven to 225 degrees Fahrenheit and place a sheet pan lined with foil on center rack.

Using the same sauté pan, heat the pan for 1–2 minutes. Add ½ tablespoon of clarified butter and swirl to coat the bottom of the pan. Using 1 heaping tablespoon per pancake, spoon the batter into the pan to form 2- to 2½-inch pancakes. Cook in batches of 4 over medium heat for 1½ minutes or until pancakes are browned around the edges. Use a thin metal spatula to loosen pancakes and turn them over. Pat them down and cook for about 1½ minutes. Remove the pancakes to warm oven. Continue cooking in batches until there are 16 pancakes, using clarified butter as needed to coat the bottom of the pan.

TO ASSEMBLE

On a warm serving tray arrange potato pancakes and add 1 teaspoon dollop of Chive Cream on top of each pancake. Gently place a salmon rosette on top of Chive Cream and sprinkle Wheat Berry Caviar around the edges of each pancake. Alternately, serve 2 salmon rosette pancakes per person and garnish plates with Wheat Berry Caviar and snipped chives. Serve immediately.

FOR THE POTATO PANCAKES

4 tablespoons clarified butter
½ cup minced onion
1 peeled, finely grated Idaho potato
2 teaspoons lemon juice
2 tablespoons flour
1 egg
⅓ cup chopped chives
1 teaspoon minced garlic
½ teaspoon salt

FOR THE POTATOES

8 new potatoes, no larger than 1½
* inches each*
salt, freshly ground black pepper

FOR THE SALAD FILLING

1 cup finely diced, cooked lobster meat
* (see note)*
¼ cup diced and rendered pancetta or
* blanched and rendered smoked*
* bacon*
1 tablespoon finely chopped scallions
½ teaspoon chopped chervil
1 teaspoon Dijon mustard
1 tablespoon olive oil
1 tablespoon lemon juice
1 teaspoon minced onion
1 teaspoon Agrumato Lemon Oil
* (see note) or ½ teaspoon grated*
* lemon rind*
salt, freshly ground black pepper
chervil sprigs, as garnish

〜 NOTES

Any type of small potato, such as Red
Bliss, works well for this recipe.

A 1¼-pound lobster yields about ½
cup diced, cooked claw and tail meat.

Agrumato Lemon Oil may be found
at gourmet food markets.

new potatoes
with lobster and bacon

An unusual but pleasing combination of ingredients will delight your guests.

YIELD: 16 STUFFED POTATO HALVES

POTATOES

Preheat oven to 375 degrees Fahrenheit.

Rinse off potatoes and trim away any nubs or black spots. Cut potatoes in half and use a melon baller to scoop out the center of each potato. Trim a small slice from the bottom of each potato so they don't roll over. In a medium-size saucepan fitted with a lid bring about 8 cups of water to a boil. Add potatoes and cook for 5 minutes with lid on. Drain the potatoes and cool 10 minutes. Arrange potatoes on a sheet pan lined with foil and season with salt and freshly ground black pepper. Bake for 25–30 minutes or until potatoes are just tender and golden in color. Allow to cool 15 minutes or to room temperature.

SALAD FILLING

YIELD: 1½ CUPS

In a medium-size bowl combine the lobster meat and pancetta with the scallions and chervil. Add the mustard, olive oil, and lemon juice and toss with lobster. Sprinkle in the onion, add the Agrumato Lemon Oil, and season with salt and freshly ground black pepper. Gently mix the filling, spoon about 1 tablespoon into each potato half, and garnish with a sprig of chervil.

caramel pork
with raisin dressing baked in crust

Bite-sized buns with an Asian flavor.

Yield: 25 buns

CARAMEL PORK FILLING

Yield: 1½ cups

Plumping the raisins in grappa may be done 1 day in advance.

In a small saucepan combine the raisins with enough water to cover, bring to a boil, cook for 1 minute, drain, and remove to a bowl. Add the grappa to warm raisins and allow to soak for at least 1 hour. Once the raisins have plumped up, reserve about 1 tablespoon, or about 25 raisins, for garnishing, and use the remaining raisins for the filling.

In a heavy-bottomed, medium-size saucepan with a fitted lid combine the pork, garlic, shallots, and sugar. Toss to combine, then add the tamari, fish sauce, and lime juice. Bring the pork mixture up to a simmer, stirring a few times. Then cover and cook the pork over low heat for 30 minutes, stirring occasionally. Remove the lid and continue cooking over low heat for 5 minutes to reduce the juices in the bottom of the pan so mixture is almost dry. Remove to a bowl to cool. When the pork mixture is cool add the chiffonade of herbs, the jalapeño, raisins, lime juice, and olive oil. Toss to combine, cover, and refrigerate until ready to form pork buns.

CRUST

Yield: 28 ounces dough

In the work bowl of a food processor fitted with a metal blade, combine the flour and salt and pulse a few seconds. Add the butter and pulse until

FOR THE FILLING

¼ cup plus 1 tablespoon raisins

¼ cup grappa or brandy

½ pound finely diced fresh pork butt or shoulder

2 tablespoons minced garlic

2 tablespoons minced shallot

1 tablespoon sugar

1 tablespoon tamari (see note)

1 tablespoon Asian fish sauce, optional (see note)

1 tablespoon lime juice

¼ cup chiffonade of cilantro

¼ cup chiffonade of scallion

¼ cup chiffonade of Thai basil (see note)

1 tablespoon minced jalapeño pepper

1 tablespoon lime juice

1 tablespoon olive oil

FOR THE CRUST

3½ cups flour

1 teaspoon salt

½ pound cold unsalted butter, cut into ½-inch pieces

1 large whole egg

1 egg yolk

3 tablespoons ice water

Tamari is similar to soy sauce but is thicker with a mellow flavor.

Fish sauce can be found in Asian markets, at health food stores, or with the Thai food products in some supermarkets.

Chiffonade is a French term used to describe thin strips or shreds of herbs or vegetables.

Thai basil has darker leaves and a stronger flavor than Italian basil. Italian basil can be substituted for Thai basil.

FOR THE GLAZE

¼ cup sugar

¼ cup water

1 tablespoon tamari

1 tablespoon molasses

the mixture resembles coarse crumbs. Remove the flour mixture to a large bowl.

In a small bowl combine the egg, egg yolk, and ice water and mix well. In a stream, slowly pour the egg mixture into the flour mixture, stirring until the flour is coming together and grainy-looking. Press the dough mixture together into a ball. Do not work dough. Cut the ball in half and flatten into 2 disks. Cover with plastic wrap and chill for 45 minutes.

On a floured surface roll out the dough ¼ inch thick. Using a 3-inch round cutter, cut out rounds of dough. Each batch of dough will yield between 8–10 rounds. Flouring the surface and rolling pin, roll out each round to about 4 inches across and ⅛ inch thick.

Placing round in palm of hand, spoon in 1 level tablespoon of filling. Fold up sides of round and pinch together dough to seal in filling. Place pinched end down on a parchment-lined sheet pan. Continue until the pan is filled with about 8–10 buns, then chill buns for 30 minutes. Reserve any dough scraps and chill. Repeat the process with second batch of dough. Again, reserve any dough scraps and combine. Roll out dough and repeat process for a total of 25 buns. Alternatively, this recipe can be baked as a roll like a strudel and sliced when cool.

Preheat oven to 350 degrees Fahrenheit.

GLAZE

In a 1-quart saucepan combine the sugar and water and bring to a boil. Stir to dissolve sugar. Remove the syrup from heat and stir in the tamari and molasses. Remove to a bowl.

Bake buns for 30 minutes or until crust is set and bottoms have just browned. Remove hot buns to a tray lined with a cooling rack. Using a pastry brush, coat the hot buns with warm glaze. Allow to dry for a minute and brush on another coat of glaze. Top each bun with a raisin soaked in grappa and serve immediately.

cajun seared scallops
with root vegetable slaw
and old bay biscuits

nspired by the flavors and classic recipes of the Louisiana shore, spicy scallops and bacon-dressed slaw are piled on tender biscuits.

Serves 8

CAJUN SPICE MIX

Combine all ingredients in a small bowl. Store Cajun Spice Mix in an airtight container until ready to use. It will keep indefinitely.

CAJUN SPREAD

The Cajun Spread may be made 1 day in advance and stored in the refrigerator.

In a small bowl combine all ingredients, mix well, and adjust seasoning with salt. Cover with plastic wrap and chill for 1–2 hours to blend flavors.

BACON DRESSING

Cook the bacon in a medium-size sauté pan over low heat for 5–6 minutes or until crisp. Remove the bacon from the pan, leaving the fat, and drain on paper towels. To the bacon fat add the vinegar, sugar, salt, and freshly ground black pepper. Stir the mixture until sugar dissolves, then remove from pan to a medium-size bowl. Add the herbs to the dressing and mix well.

FOR THE CAJUN SPICE MIX

2 tablespoons paprika
2 tablespoons cayenne pepper
1½ tablespoons fine sea salt
1 tablespoon onion powder
1 tablespoon garlic powder
2 teaspoons ground white pepper
2¼ teaspoons freshly ground black pepper
2¼ teaspoons dried thyme leaves, crumbled
2¼ teaspoons dried oregano, crumbled

FOR THE CAJUN SPREAD

½ cup mayonnaise
2 tablespoons lemon juice
1 tablespoon Cajun Spice Mix
1 tablespoon chopped cilantro
1 teaspoon minced garlic
salt

FOR THE BACON DRESSING

6 slices finely chopped smoked bacon
4 tablespoons cider vinegar
1½ teaspoons sugar
salt, freshly ground black pepper
2 tablespoons chopped parsley
1 tablespoon chopped basil

FOR THE SLAW

½ cup finely shredded carrot
½ cup finely shredded turnip
½ cup finely shredded parsnip
½ cup finely shredded rutabaga
½ cup finely shredded celery root
  or knob

FOR THE BISCUITS

2 cups flour
1 tablespoon baking powder
1 teaspoon sugar
1 teaspoon baking soda
1 teaspoon salt
1¼ teaspoons Old Bay Seasoning
6 tablespoons (¾ stick) chilled butter,
  cut in ½-inch pieces
4 tablespoons chilled vegetable
  shortening
¾ cup buttermilk plus 1 tablespoon for
  brushing
1 tablespoon melted butter

FOR THE SCALLOPS

1 pound diver or very large sea scallops
  (about 8–10 scallops)
1–2 tablespoons Cajun Spice Mix
2–3 tablespoons olive oil

ROOT VEGETABLE SLAW

Pour the dressing over the shredded vegetables and toss to coat. Add the bacon, mix well, and adjust the seasoning with salt and freshly ground black pepper if necessary. Chill the slaw until ready to serve.

OLD BAY BISCUITS

*Y*IELD: 16 BISCUITS

Preheat oven to 400 degrees Fahrenheit.

In the work bowl of a food processor fitted with a metal blade, combine the dry ingredients by pulsing several times. Add the butter and shortening and pulse 10–12 times or until mixture resembles coarse meal. Place the mixture in a large bowl.

Make a well in the center of the flour mixture and add ¾ cup buttermilk. Stir with a wooden spoon until the mixture forms a dough. Do not overmix. Turn the dough out onto a lightly floured surface. Gently knead the dough 8–10 times. Roll out dough to ¾-inch thickness.

Cut the dough with a 2-inch biscuit cutter. Place the biscuits on an insulated cookie sheet about ½ inch apart. The closer together the biscuits, the higher they will rise when baked. Gently form dough scraps together, roll out, and cut additional biscuits. Brush the tops of biscuits lightly with buttermilk and bake for 12–15 minutes or until golden brown. Remove the biscuits to a cooling rack, brush with melted butter, and cool to room temperature.

CAJUN SEARED SCALLOPS

Cut the scallops into ¼-inch-thick slices. Sprinkle both sides of scallops with seasoning mix. Preheat a large nonstick sauté pan over high heat for 2–3 minutes.

(continues)

Add a small amount of olive oil and swirl to coat the bottom of the pan. In batches of about 8–10 slices, sear the scallops for 10–15 seconds on each side. The scallops should be lightly browned, but be careful not to overcook them.

TO ASSEMBLE

Cut each biscuit in half, keeping bottoms and tops separate. Cover each half biscuit with 1 teaspoon Cajun Spread. On the bottom halves, arrange a small amount of Root Vegetable Slaw, 2–3 seared scallop slices, and a small amount more of slaw. Gently add the top half of each biscuit and serve immediately.

$\mathcal{S}$OUPS AND SALADS

Puree of Butternut Squash and Granny Smith Apple
with Timbale of Leek, Apple, and Pancetta

Hot Pumpkin Soup with Country Bacon,
Goat Cheese Gnocchi,
and Wild Mushroom Sauté with Spinach Cream

Young Greens with Hazelnut Dressing,
Oven-Roasted Tomatoes,
and Maytag Blue Cheese Spoon Bread

puree of butternut squash
and granny smith apple
with timbale of leek, apple, and pancetta

 *silky smooth soup accented by sweet-tart apple and crisp bacon.*

Serves 8

SOUP

This soup stores well and can be prepared 2 days ahead to the point of assembling the timbales, which should be assembled just before the soup is served. Store the puree and the finished soup in the refrigerator in airtight containers.

Preheat oven to 350 degrees Fahrenheit.

Cut the butternut squash in half crosswise, and reserve the top half of 1 squash for the timbale garnish. Cut remaining 3 pieces of squash in half lengthwise and remove the seeds. Place the squash, skin-side down, in a shallow roasting pan, brush with 1½ tablespoons melted butter, and season with salt and freshly ground black pepper. Roast for 1 hour or until the squash is tender when pierced with the tip of a sharp knife. Allow the squash to cool to room temperature.

When the squash is cool scoop the insides from skin and place in the work bowl of a food processor fitted with a metal blade. Puree the squash until smooth. Reserve 1 cup of squash puree for the timbale. Place the remaining puree in a large bowl, cover with plastic wrap, and set aside.

Peel and core the apples and cut into ½-inch-thick wedges. Heat the remaining 1½ tablespoons butter in large, nonstick skillet over medium-high heat. Add

FOR THE SOUP

2 butternut squash, approximately
 1½ pounds each
3 tablespoons butter, melted
salt, freshly ground black pepper
2 Granny Smith apples
½ cup Riesling wine
3 ounces finely diced pancetta
1 cup thinly sliced leeks (see note)
½ cup thinly sliced shallots
½ cup thinly sliced carrots
½ cup thinly sliced celery
6 cups chicken or vegetable stock

NOTES

Butternut squash puree is used both for the soup and the Timbale of Leek, Apple, and Pancetta. The timbale also includes finely diced and sautéed butternut squash.

To clean the leeks, split in half lengthwise and cut halves into thin strips. Soak in cool water for 10 minutes. Gently shake off the excess water and cut the leek strips into a fine dice. Wash the diced leek in standing water to get rid of any remaining sand or grit. Lift the leeks out of the water and drain in a fine-mesh strainer.

FOR THE TIMBALE

1 cup finely diced butternut squash

2 tablespoons butter

1 cup finely chopped leeks (see note)

1 cup peeled, finely chopped Granny Smith apple tossed with 1 tablespoon lemon juice

½ cup Riesling wine

1 cup reserved butternut squash puree (see note)

⅓ cup reserved, cooked pancetta bacon (see above)

¼ cup finely chopped chives

freshly ground black pepper

apple wedges and cook for 8–10 minutes or until lightly browned and tender. Add the wine and continue cooking until the wine reduces and the mixture is almost dry. Remove the cooked apple wedges from heat and set aside with the squash puree.

Wipe out the skillet and cook the diced pancetta over low heat, stirring frequently, until crisp. Remove crisp pancetta, drain on paper towels, and reserve for the timbale garnish. Discard all but 1 tablespoon of fat from the skillet, raise the heat to medium, add the leeks, shallots, carrots, and celery, and season the vegetables with salt and freshly ground black pepper. Mix the vegetables, cover with a lid or foil, and turn down the heat to low. Cook the mixture for 10 minutes, stirring occasionally. Add the chicken stock, cover, and cook for an additional 10–15 minutes or until vegetables are tender. Add the reserved squash puree and apples, bring to a boil, and cook for 5 minutes.

Fill a food processor halfway to avoid overflowing hot soup, and puree the soup in several batches. Ladle the soup through a fine-mesh strainer into a clean pot. The soup can be kept warm while the timbale garnish is prepared. If the soup is made ahead of serving time, allow it to cool to room temperature, then store it in the refrigerator in an airtight container.

FOR THE TIMBALE

Peel the remaining half squash and cut into a very fine dice.

Heat a medium-size, nonstick skillet over medium heat for 2 minutes. Add 2 tablespoons butter and swirl to coat the bottom of the pan. Add the leeks and cook for 4 minutes, stirring occasionally. Add squash and cook for 4 minutes, continuing to stir the mixture occasionally. Add apple, cook for 2 minutes, then add the wine and cook until the wine reduces and the mixture is almost dry. Remove the timbale garnish from the pan, set aside, and keep warm until serving soup.

(continues)

puree of butternut squash, *continued*

TO SERVE SOUP

Place the squash puree reserved for the timbale in a microwave-safe glass dish, cover with waxed paper, and heat on high for 1–2 minutes or until hot. In a medium-size saucepan bring the soup to a simmer over low heat, stirring frequently.

Lay out 8 warmed soup plates. To make the timbales, place a small scoop of hot squash puree into the center of each soup plate. Flatten each scoop of puree with the back of a spoon and top with ¼ cup warm timbale garnish. Ladle the soup around each timbale, then sprinkle with pancetta, chives, and a grind of black pepper. Serve immediately.

hot pumpkin soup
with country bacon, goat cheese gnocchi, and wild mushroom sauté with spinach cream

⁓ **NOTE**

If fresh pumpkin is not available, this soup can be prepared with calabaza squash, a variety of pumpkin from the West Indies.

This rich soup, perfect as a starter for a winter dinner, has an added bonus: when you make the gnocchi garnish, there will be enough left over to serve two for another dinner.

Serves 8

HOT PUMPKIN SOUP WITH COUNTRY BACON

Yield: 8 cups

This soup stores well and can be prepared 2 days ahead of serving.

Preheat oven to 375 degrees Fahrenheit.

Split the pumpkin in half crosswise and remove the seeds. Place the pumpkin into a shallow roasting pan, skin-side down, drizzle with olive oil, and season with salt and freshly ground black pepper. Pour ½ cup water into the bottom of the pan. Roast the pumpkin for 45–60 minutes or until the pumpkin is tender when pierced with the tip of a sharp knife. Remove the pumpkin from the oven and cool to room temperature. When cool, scoop the pumpkin from the skin. There should be 1½–1¾ pounds of roasted pumpkin.

In a large, heavy-bottomed pot, cook the diced bacon for 7–8 minutes over very low heat, stirring frequently until crisp. Remove the crisp bacon and reserve for garnishing the Goat Cheese Gnocchi. Discard all but 1 tablespoon of fat from

(continues)

hot pumpkin soup, *continued*

FOR THE GNOCCHI

2 Idaho potatoes, scrubbed

1 teaspoon olive oil

½ cup minced onion

3 tablespoons reserved cooked bacon, finely chopped

2 tablespoons reserved spinach puree

1 teaspoon salt

5–6 ounces fresh goat cheese, crumbled

1 egg, lightly beaten

1½ cups flour, plus additional for dusting

salt to taste

2 teaspoons olive oil

the pan and over medium-low heat add the onion and leeks and cook for 5–6 minutes or until translucent. Add the carrots and cook for an additional 5–6 minutes, stirring occasionally. Add the garlic and cook for 1 minute, stirring constantly. Add the roasted pumpkin, chicken stock, thyme, and bay leaf. Mix the soup and raise heat to medium. Bring the soup to a boil, stirring frequently so pumpkin doesn't settle to the bottom of the pot and burn. Once the soup is boiling reduce the heat slightly and simmer for 45–50 minutes.

Allow the soup to cool slightly. Fill the jar of a blender halfway to avoid overflowing hot soup, and puree the soup in several batches. Ladle the soup through a fine-mesh strainer, discarding any solids, and place in a clean pot. Reheat the soup when ready to serve. If the soup is made ahead of time, allow it to cool to room temperature, then store it in the refrigerator in an airtight container.

GOAT CHEESE GNOCCHI

Place the potatoes in a medium-size pot with a fitted lid. Fill the pot with water until the water is 1 inch above the top of the potatoes, and bring to a boil on high heat. Reduce the heat to low and cover, leaving the lid ajar to prevent water from boiling over. Simmer for 25–30 minutes or until the potatoes are tender when pierced with the tip of a sharp knife. Remove the potatoes from the pot and allow them to cool for 20–25 minutes.

While potatoes are cooling, heat olive oil in a small sauté pan over low heat for 1 minute, add the onions, and cook for 6–7 minutes or until translucent. Stir occasionally. Allow to cool to room temperature.

Peel the potatoes and grate them into a large bowl, using the coarse side of box grater. Add the cooled onion, reserved bacon, and reserved spinach puree to the grated potatoes and mix well with a wooden spoon. Add salt and crumbled goat cheese. Mix until smooth and the goat cheese is blended into potato. Add

FOR THE WILD MUSHROOM SAUTÉ

8–10 ounces wild mushrooms (see note)
4 tablespoons unsalted butter
⅓ cup minced shallots
¼ teaspoon minced garlic
salt, freshly ground black pepper
24–32 pieces of reserved cooked gnocchi

⁓ NOTES

This recipe makes enough gnocchi to garnish the pumpkin soup and serve 2 dinner or 4 appetizer portions on another occasion. Top the gnocchi with your favorite pasta sauce and crumbled goat cheese.

When shaping the gnocchi, practice with the same few pieces of dough to master the technique. When rolling the gnocchi dough into shapes, try not to incorporate too much flour into the dough.

A combination of black trumpet, oyster, shiitake, chanterelle, or enoki mushrooms will work well for this recipe, or use your favorite combination of wild mushrooms. Wild mushrooms can be purchased in most gourmet food markets and in some supermarkets.

egg and mix until incorporated. Add 1 cup of flour and mix until a sticky dough is formed.

Sprinkle remaining ½ cup flour on flat surface. Turn the dough onto the flour and knead dough until flour is incorporated. Cut the dough into 6 pieces and dust lightly with flour. On a lightly floured surface roll a piece of dough into a rope about 1 inch in diameter. Cut the rope into ¾- inch-long pieces. With floured hands roll the pieces into balls. Using a ridged wooden paddle (the tool used for rolling butter balls), or the smooth side of a handheld cheese grater held at a 45-degree angle, roll the dough with your index and middle finger from the top to bottom and allow the gnocchi to drop. This motion is the shape of a cursive letter *C.* The dough should have a slight indentation and look like a rolled scroll. Practice on a few pieces of dough and then finish shaping gnocchi. In a single layer, place the gnocchi on a sheet pan lined with waxed paper and cook soon after shaping.

Bring large pot of water to a boil. Add 2–3 tablespoons salt or to taste. Add 10–15 pieces of gnocchi to the boiling water. Let the gnocchi cook until they rise to surface and then continue cooking for an additional minute. Lift the gnocchi out of water with a slotted spoon. Cool the gnocchi in ice water for 1 minute, then place them in colander to drain. When all gnocchi are cooked and drained, place them in a large bowl and toss with 2 teaspoons olive oil. Reserve about 3-4 gnocchi per person to serve with the pumpkin soup. Store the gnocchi in an airtight container in refrigerator for up to 2 days.

WILD MUSHROOM SAUTÉ

Wash the wild mushrooms in standing water briefly, just to remove grit. Allow the mushrooms to drain in a colander and then trim tough stems. Thinly slice mushrooms.

(continues)

hot pumpkin soup, *continued*

FOR THE SPINACH CREAM
½ pound spinach leaves
¾ cup heavy cream, reduced to ½ cup
salt, freshly ground black pepper

Preheat a large nonstick sauté pan over medium heat for 2–3 minutes, then add 2 tablespoons butter. Allow the butter to foam, then add the shallots and garlic, and cook for 4–5 minutes, stirring frequently, taking care not to brown shallots. Add the mushrooms and cook for 4–5 minutes or until mushrooms are just starting to brown. Season with salt and freshly ground black pepper. Then cook for an additional 4–5 minutes or until the mushrooms are golden brown. Scrape the Wild Mushroom Sauté into a small bowl and set aside.

Add the remaining 2 tablespoons butter to the sauté pan and allow the butter to foam, add the gnocchi, and toss to coat. Reduce the heat to low and cook until gnocchi are warmed through, about 2–3 minutes, stirring once or twice. Return the mushrooms to pan and mix with gnocchi to reheat. Prepare to serve soup.

SPINACH CREAM

Y IELD: ⅔ CUP

The Spinach Cream can be prepared 3–4 hours ahead of serving time.

Wash the spinach leaves several times to remove sand and grit. Lift out of standing water. Place wet spinach leaves in a large pot with a tight-fitting lid. Season spinach with salt, cover, and cook over high heat for 1 minute, stir once, and cook for an additional 1–2 minutes or until spinach wilts. Place the spinach in ice water to stop the cooking and retain the bright green color, then remove to a colander to drain.

Squeeze any remaining water from spinach and place in the work bowl of food processor fitted with a metal blade. Puree the spinach, scraping down sides of the work bowl as necessary. Reserve 2 tablespoons of spinach puree for the Goat Cheese Gnocchi.

Add reduced cream to the remaining spinach and pulse several times to blend. Process the mixture for 30–40 seconds to puree and pour into 1-cup glass measure. Season the Spinach Cream with salt and freshly ground black pepper, cover with plastic wrap, and refrigerate. To serve with the soup, microwave Spinach Cream on high for 30–45 seconds or until steaming.

TO SERVE

Bring the soup to a simmer. Lay out 8 warmed, shallow soup plates and spoon 3 or 4 warm Goat Cheese Gnocchi and some Wild Mushroom Sauté in center of each plate. Carefully ladle soup into bowls, drizzle with Spinach Cream, and serve immediately.

Served at the Fulbright Dinner, this first course is a combination of uniquely American ingredients and flavors. The plate is from the Theodore Roosevelt state china service.

8 ripe Roma or plum tomatoes

1½ tablespoons balsamic vinegar

1½ tablespoons olive oil

2 teaspoons minced garlic

2 tablespoons chopped basil

salt, freshly ground black pepper

FOR THE GREENS

½ pound baby field greens

2 ounces peppercress sprouts (see note)

2 ounces corn sprouts

2 cups mâche, lamb's tongue lettuce

FOR THE DRESSING

2 tablespoons minced shallots

½ teaspoon minced garlic

salt, freshly ground black pepper

2 tablespoons Dijon mustard

1 tablespoon lemon juice

¼ cup hazelnut oil

1 tablespoon champagne vinegar

¼ cup olive oil

1 tablespoon chopped chives

1 tablespoon chopped tarragon leaves

1 cup toasted hazelnuts, chopped

⌒ **NOTE**

If peppercress and corn sprouts are not available, substitute alfalfa, broccoli, pea sprouts, or radish sprouts.

young greens
with hazelnut dressing, oven-roasted tomatoes, and maytag blue cheese spoon bread

*S*ERVES 8

OVEN-ROASTED TOMATOES

Preheat oven to 200 degrees Fahrenheit.

Line a 10 x 15-inch jelly roll pan with foil. Place a wire rack in the pan. Cut the tomatoes in half lengthwise and place cut-side up on rack.

In a small bowl combine the vinegar, olive oil, and garlic and mix well. Drizzle the mixture over the tomatoes and sprinkle with the chopped basil, salt, and freshly ground black pepper. Place the tomatoes in the oven for 4–5 hours or until slightly dry and firm. Allow the tomatoes to cool to room temperature and peel. Serve 2 halves with each salad.

YOUNG GREENS

Gently wash the baby field greens and sprouts and drain in a colander. Place the greens and sprouts in a large bowl and toss gently to combine. Wash the mâche separately and reserve for sprinkling on salad just before serving. Cover all the greens and refrigerate.

DRESSING

*Y*IELD: ⅔ CUP DRESSING

In a small bowl combine shallots, garlic, salt, and freshly ground black pepper. Mix well and allow to sit for 4–5 minutes so the juices come out of shallots.

(continues)

young greens, *continued*

Add the mustard and lemon juice and mix well. Whisking the mixture, slowly add the hazelnut oil, vinegar, and olive oil. Add chopped herbs and check the seasoning. Set aside until ready to toss salad.

MAYTAG BLUE CHEESE SPOON BREAD

Preheat oven to 375 degrees Fahrenheit.

Butter an 8-cup, straight-sided casserole or soufflé dish and set aside.

In a large, heavy-bottomed pot, bring the water and salt to a boil. Slowly whisk in the cornmeal and grits. Reduce the heat to very low and cook the mixture for 15 minutes, stirring frequently with a wooden spoon. The mixture will be very thick. Remove the pot from heat and cool for 15–20 minutes, stirring frequently.

When the cornmeal mixture has cooled, mix in the cream and butter. Add the baking powder and egg yolks. In a medium-size bowl whip the egg whites with a handheld mixer on high for 2 minutes or until soft white peaks form. Gently fold the egg whites into the cornmeal batter. Fold in the cheese and pour the batter into buttered baking dish. Bake for 40–45 minutes or until the spoon bread is well browned and puffed to top of baking dish. Allow the spoon bread to cool for 15–20 minutes before serving. The spoon bread will drop slightly as it cools.

TO ASSEMBLE

Toss the field greens, except the mâche, with the dressing. Arrange dressed greens on each plate and sprinkle with mâche leaves. Place 2 tomato halves on each plate and a scoop of warm spoon bread to the side of the greens and tomatoes. Sprinkle with chopped hazelnuts and serve immediately.

FOR THE SPOON BREAD

2½ cups water

½ teaspoon salt

1 cup yellow cornmeal

¼ cup white grits (not *quick cooking*)

1 cup heavy cream

4 tablespoons butter, room temperature

2 teaspoons baking powder

3 eggs, separated

1 cup crumbled Maytag blue cheese

NOTE

When cornmeal and grits are cooking they tend to bubble and "spit," which can cause a bad burn to a hand.

ENTRÉES

Country Sausages with Peppers and Leeks

Grilled Bison Filet with Spring Vegetables, Crimini Mushroom Sauté,
and Cabernet Sauce

Pine Nut–Crusted Racks of Lamb with Olives and Oyster Mushroom Ragout

Walnut-Crusted Chicken with Crabmeat, Gruyère Cheese, and Spinach Stuffing

Black-Eyed Pea and Sweet Potato Salad

Honey-Mango-Glazed Chicken with Spicy Vegetable "Noodles" and Herb Tuile

Grilled Shrimp and Smoked Chicken with Creole Couscous
and Tart Apple and Scallion Coulis

Poached Lobster with Marinated Orange Salad,
Saffron-Scented Basmati Rice,
and Emerald Cilantro Chutney

country sausages
with peppers and leeks

An herbed topping of peppers, leeks, onions, and garlic changes store-bought sausages into something very special.

Serves 8

TO PREPARE PEPPER AND LEEKS

Toss the garlic cloves with 1 teaspoon olive oil. Wrap loosely in foil and roast in 375-degree oven for 45 minutes or until cloves are soft to the touch. Allow the roasted cloves to cool, then peel and remove the hard stem ends.

Roast the peppers over an open flame or under a broiler until skins are charred. Place the roasted peppers in a paper bag to steam for 10 minutes. Peel and cut peppers into ¼-inch-wide strips.

To clean the leeks, split in half lengthwise and soak in cool water for 10 minutes. Gently shake off the excess water and cut leeks into 2 x ¼-inch strips, or about the same size as the pepper strips. Wash the leek strips in standing water to get rid of any remaining sand or grit. Lift the leek strips out of the water and drain in a colander until almost dry.

Heat 3 tablespoons olive oil in a large nonstick sauté pan over medium-high heat for 2 minutes. Add the sliced onion and cook for 5–6 minutes or until translucent and wilted. Add the leek strips, season with salt and freshly ground black pepper, and cook for an additional 8–10 minutes or until caramelized, stirring occasionally.

24 unpeeled garlic cloves

3 tablespoons plus 1 teaspoon
    olive oil

2 red bell peppers

2 yellow bell peppers

2 green bell peppers

2–3 large leeks, white part only

1 large onion, sliced

salt, freshly ground black pepper

2 tablespoons chopped basil

2 teaspoons chopped oregano

1 tablespoon Agrumato Lemon Oil
    (see note)

2 tablespoons balsamic vinegar

4–5 pounds or 24 assorted sausages
    (see note)

~ **NOTES**

Agrumato Lemon Oil may be found in gourmet markets.

This recipe works well with a variety of bratwurst, weisswurst, country-style, and knockwurst sausages.

Add the pepper strips, peeled garlic, and herbs to the onions and leeks. Mix gently and cook until mixture is warmed through. Remove the vegetables from heat and mix in the Agrumato Lemon Oil and balsamic vinegar. Season to taste with salt and freshly ground pepper. Keep warm.

TO PREPARE SAUSAGES

Pierce each sausage with the tip of a sharp knife 3—4 times. Blanch any raw, country-style sausages before grilling.

Prepare grill, brush the sausages lightly with oil, and grill until nicely browned and cooked through. Allow the sausages to rest 10 minutes. When serving, sausages may be cut in half so guests can try several varieties. Serve the warm peppers and caramelized leeks over top of sausages.

grilled bison filet

with spring vegetables, crimini mushroom sauté, and cabernet sauce

Farm-raised bison has a rich, beefy flavor but is lower in fat. Use a good California cabernet for the sauce.

Serves 8

CABERNET SAUCE

The Cabernet Sauce can be prepared up to 2 days in advance; wait until reheating the sauce to finish it with butter.

Heat a large sauce pot over medium heat for 1–2 minutes. Add 2 tablespoons butter and cook until it foams. Add shallots and cook for 1–2 minutes, stirring constantly. Add mushrooms, toss to coat with butter, and cook for 7–8 minutes or until lightly browned. Add peppercorns and wine and bring to a boil. Reduce heat to medium low and simmer for 15–20 minutes or until reduced to ⅔ cup. Add demi-glace and bring to a boil on medium low and simmer for 20–25 minutes or until sauce coats the back of a spoon. Strain sauce through a fine-mesh strainer into a clean, medium-size sauce pot. Bring to a simmer over medium heat, skimming any foam that rises. Adjust the seasoning, turn off heat, and whisk in the remaining butter. Keep the sauce warm until ready to serve.

CRIMINI MUSHROOM SAUTÉ

The Crimini Mushroom Sauté can be prepared 2–3 hours ahead and reheated when ready to serve.

To clean the leeks, split in half lengthwise and soak in cool water for 10 minutes. Gently shake off the excess water and thinly slice the leeks. Wash the leek slices in standing water to get rid of any remaining sand or grit. Lift the sliced leeks out of the water and drain in a colander.

FOR THE CABERNET SAUCE

3 tablespoons unsalted butter
½ cup finely chopped shallots
1 cup chopped mushroom stems
6 cracked black peppercorns
3 cups Cabernet Sauvignon wine
4 cups demi-glace

FOR THE SAUTÉ

4 cups sliced leeks
4 tablespoons unsalted butter
4 cups stemmed and quartered crimini mushrooms
2 cups sliced endive
salt, freshly ground black pepper
½ cup dry white wine

～ NOTES

Demi-glace, a classic sauce for meats, is available in gourmet markets.

Bison or buffalo is a lean meat. To keep the meat tender and moist, cook it rare to medium rare.

FOR THE BISON WITH VEGETABLES

3 bunches baby carrots, tops trimmed, washed and peeled

½ pound haricots verts

1 bunch asparagus

24 (1-inch) Yukon Gold potatoes, scrubbed

16 pieces yellow patty pan squash

8 (6- or 7-ounce) bison filets or sirloin strip steaks

salt, freshly ground black pepper

8 teaspoons olive oil

4 tablespoons unsalted butter

Heat a large nonstick sauté pan over medium-high heat for 2–3 minutes. Add the butter and cook just until butter starts to brown. Add the mushrooms, toss them in the pan to coat with butter, and cook for 2 minutes, tossing occasionally. Add the leeks and endive to the mushrooms. Season the mixture with salt and freshly ground black pepper and cook for 7–8 minutes or until mushrooms are golden brown. Add the wine and cook for 2–3 minutes or until the mixture is almost dry. Place the Crimini Mushroom Sauté in a small bowl and set aside in a warm place if serving immediately. If Crimini Mushroom Sauté is prepared a few hours in advance, store it in the refrigerator until ready to reheat.

GRILLED BISON FILET WITH SPRING VEGETABLES

The vegetables in this recipe should be prepared separately, as cooking times vary. When ready to serve, sauté the vegetables together in butter to heat through.

The vegetables can be prepared 3–4 hours ahead of serving time and stored in the refrigerator.

BABY CARROTS

Steam the baby carrots for 5–6 minutes or until tender crisp and then plunge them into ice water. When the carrots are cool remove them to a colander to drain and then place them in a large bowl.

HARICOTS VERTS

Trim the stem ends of haricots verts and steam for 4–5 minutes or until tender crisp, then plunge them into ice water. When the beans are cool remove them to a colander to drain and add them to the carrots.

ASPARAGUS

Trim the stem ends of the asparagus and steam for 4–5 minutes or until tender crisp, then plunge them into ice water. When the asparagus are cool remove them to a colander to drain and combine with steamed vegetables.

(continues)

grilled bison filet, *continued*

YUKON GOLD POTATOES

Steam the potatoes for 8–10 minutes or until tender when pierced with the tip of a small sharp knife. Remove them to a colander to drain and cool.

PATTY PAN

Steam the squash for 2–3 minutes or until tender crisp when pierced with the tip of a small sharp knife. Plunge the squash into ice water. When the squash are cool remove them to a colander to drain and combine with steamed vegetables.

The asparagus, potatoes, and patty pan may be cut in half when cooled, if smaller pieces are desired. Reserve the vegetables. When ready to grill the bison filets have the Cabernet Sauce and Crimini Mushroom Sauté prepared.

Season the meat with salt and freshly ground black pepper and brush each filet with 1 teaspoon olive oil. Heat a grill pan over medium-high heat for 5–6 minutes or until a drop of water evaporates on contact. Alternately, prepare a barbecue according to the manufacturer's directions. Cook the filets for 4–5 minutes on each side for medium rare to rare. Keep the grilled filets warm while finishing the vegetables.

Heat a large-size sauté pan over high heat for 1–2 minutes. Add 4 tablespoons butter and allow the butter to foam. Add the vegetables and toss them in the pan until well coated with butter and evenly heated. Season with salt and freshly ground black pepper. Add 1–2 tablespoons water to the sauté pan and toss the vegetables again; this will make a buttery sauce to coat the vegetables.

TO ASSEMBLE

Place a small spoonful of warm mushroom mixture on each warmed dinner plate, top with a Grilled Bison Filet, and arrange the Spring Vegetables around each filet. Drizzle 1 ounce Cabernet Sauce over each filet, and serve immediately. Serve additional vegetables and sauce at table.

FOR RACKS OF LAMB AND
PINE NUT CRUST

4 trimmed, whole racks of lamb,
    8 bones each (see note)
2 tablespoons olive oil
salt, freshly ground black pepper
2½ cups pine nuts, coarsely chopped
1 cup soft fresh bread crumbs
¼ cup chopped and pitted Arbequina
    olives (or small black olives, such as
    Kalamata)
¼ cup chopped Italian parsley
¼ cup chopped chives
1 tablespoon chopped rosemary
1 tablespoon chopped thyme leaves
1 cup honey mustard
1 tablespoon cognac

⌒ NOTE

When purchasing racks of lamb, have
butcher remove all fat and bones
except the rib bones, which are
trimmed, or "Frenched."

pine nut–crusted racks of lamb
with olives and
oyster mushroom ragout

*S*ERVES 8

RACKS OF LAMB

Preheat a large nonstick sauté pan over high heat for 1–2 minutes or until a
drop of water sizzles in pan. Brush the racks of lamb with oil and sprinkle with
salt and freshly ground black pepper. Brown the racks on all sides, taking care
not to crowd the pan. Once the racks are browned set aside to cool.

TO PREPARE PINE NUT CRUST

The pine nut crust may be prepared 1 day in advance and stored in the refrigerator in an airtight container.

Combine the chopped pine nuts, bread crumbs, olives, and herbs in a medium-
size bowl. Mix well and season with salt and freshly ground black pepper.

Preheat oven to 375 degrees Fahrenheit. Combine the mustard and cognac in a
small bowl. Brush the cooled racks with mustard and gently press about 1 cup
of pine nut mixture all over meat.

Place the pine nut–crusted racks of lamb on a wire rack in a shallow roasting
pan. Roast for about 20–23 minutes for medium rare or until crust is golden
brown and internal temperature registers 140 degrees on an instant-read
thermometer. Remove the meat to a carving board and allow it to rest for 10
minutes before carving.

(continues)

The succulent racks of lamb are best served rare to medium rare. Served as individual chops at White House receptions, this dish could grace a dinner table as an entrée. In this picture it is served on a platter from the Reagan state china service.

FOR THE RAGOUT

8 ounces oyster mushrooms

*4 tablespoons butter, room temperature,
  divided*

salt, freshly ground black pepper

¼ cup minced shallots

½ cup Madeira

2 cups demi-glace (see note)

⁓ **NOTE**

Demi-glace, a classic sauce for meats,
is available in gourmet markets.

OYSTER MUSHROOM RAGOUT

$\mathscr{S}$ERVES 8

To prepare the mushrooms, remove tough stems and discard. Pull into strands and don't chop the mushrooms; there should be approximately 2½–3 cups.

Preheat a large nonstick sauté pan over medium-high heat for 1–2 minutes, then add 3 tablespoons butter. Allow the butter to foam, then add the mushrooms and toss to coat. Cook for 5–6 minutes or until the mushrooms are lightly browned, stirring occasionally. Season with salt and freshly ground pepper. Add the shallots and cook for 2–3 minutes, stirring frequently or until the mushrooms are golden brown.

Add the Madeira to the mushroom mixture and reduce heat to low. Allow Madeira to reduce until almost evaporated, then add demi-glace and bring to a boil. Skim any foam that rises to the surface as the mushrooms continue to cook.

Finish the mushroom ragout by swirling with the remaining tablespoon of butter. Adjust seasoning if necessary.

TO SERVE

Carve each rack into 4 double chops. Serve 2 per plate with the Oyster Mushroom Ragout around the chops.

walnut-crusted chicken
with crabmeat, gruyère cheese, and spinach stuffing

These crisp, stuffed chicken rolls are kept moist by the unusual stuffing. Paired with an untraditional salad of traditional Southern ingredients, they make a delicious informal meal. The china plate in the photograph on page 264 is from the Lyndon B. Johnson state service, which is decorated with American wildflowers.

Serves 8

The china plate in the photograph on page 264

FOR THE STUFFING

1 pound lump crabmeat
1 cup coarsely grated Gruyère cheese
2 tablespoons olive oil
½ cup finely diced onion
½ teaspoon minced garlic
½ cup mayonnaise
¼ cup chopped chives
½ tablespoon lemon juice
1 teaspoon Dijon mustard
½ teaspoon Tabasco sauce
½ teaspoon Worcestershire sauce
½ pound baby spinach leaves

CRABMEAT STUFFING

Carefully remove any shells or cartilage from crabmeat, a few "lumps" at a time, placing crabmeat in a large bowl as it is cleaned. Add the Gruyère cheese and mix gently. Cover the bowl with plastic wrap and chill.

Heat olive oil in a small sauté pan over low heat for 1 minute. Add the onion and cook, stirring occasionally, for 5–6 minutes or until translucent. Add the garlic and cook for 1 minute more, stirring constantly. Allow the mixture to cool to room temperature.

In a small bowl combine the mayonnaise, chives, and cooled onion mixture. Add the lemon juice, mustard, Tabasco sauce, and Worcestershire sauce and whisk to combine. Gently fold the mayonnaise mixture into the crabmeat and cheese, taking care not to break up the chunks of crabmeat.

Wash the baby spinach leaves in standing water to remove sand and grit. Lift the spinach out of the water and place in a medium-size saucepan with a fitted lid. Cook the spinach on high heat for 1 minute, stir once, and cook an additional 1–2 minutes or until spinach wilts. Place the spinach in ice water to stop the

FOR THE SAUCE

12 large cloves of garlic, unpeeled
1 teaspoon olive oil
1 cup dry white wine
¼ cup champagne vinegar
½ cup sliced shallots
1 sprig thyme
½ small bay leaf
½ teaspoon crushed black peppercorns
¼ cup heavy cream
½ pound unsalted butter, room
    temperature
1 tablespoon lemon juice
salt, freshly ground black pepper

FOR THE CHICKEN

8 (6-ounce) boneless, skinless chicken
    breast halves (see note)
salt, freshly ground black pepper
½ cup flour
2 eggs
2 cups soft fresh bread crumbs
1 cup finely chopped walnuts
2 cups peanut oil

⌒ NOTE

When purchasing chicken for this recipe, you may have the butcher butterfly and lightly pound each chicken breast. However, these steps are easy to do at home, and directions are given in the recipe.

cooking and to retain the bright green color, then remove to a colander to drain. Squeeze out the excess water from the spinach and mix carefully into the crabmeat. Cover the stuffing with plastic wrap and chill until ready to assemble the chicken rolls.

ROASTED GARLIC SAUCE

The Roasted Garlic Sauce can be prepared 1 hour ahead of serving time. Alternately, the Roasted Garlic Sauce can be prepared while the chicken rolls are chilling, but roast the garlic beforehand.

Preheat oven to 375 degrees Fahrenheit.

On a 12-inch square of foil, drizzle garlic cloves with olive oil and wrap loosely. Bake for 40–45 minutes or until the garlic is soft. Allow the garlic to cool to room temperature, then peel the cloves and remove the hard stem ends. Set aside in a small bowl.

In a medium-size, nonreactive or stainless-steel saucepan combine wine, vinegar, shallots, thyme, bay leaf, and peppercorns. Bring the wine mixture to a boil over medium-high heat. Reduce the heat to low and simmer the mixture for 10–12 minutes or until the liquid reduces to a light syrup consistency. Add the cream and cook for 1–2 minutes. Add the roasted garlic and whisk until the mixture is smooth. Whisk in the butter over very low heat, 1 tablespoon at a time. Continue whisking the sauce with each addition of butter until all the butter has been incorporated. Finish the sauce with lemon juice and season with salt and freshly ground black pepper. Strain the garlic sauce through a fine-mesh strainer and keep warm until ready to serve.

TO BUTTERFLY CHICKEN

Lay the chicken breast on a cutting board and remove the tenderloin and any remaining sinew or fat. The tenderloin can be reserved for another use. Use a

(continues)

boning knife to cut horizontally down the length of the chicken breast, stopping about ½ inch from the opposite edge. Unfold the chicken breast to form a "butterfly."

Lay the butterflied chicken on a piece of plastic wrap and cover with second piece of wrap. Butterfly the remaining chicken breasts.

Lay out the butterflied chicken breasts on a flat surface and lightly pound each with a meat mallet or the bottom of a small, heavy pan. Place the chicken on a sheet pan and refrigerate until ready to assemble the chicken rolls.

TO ASSEMBLE CHICKEN ROLLS

Lay out the butterflied chicken, remove the top plastic wrap, and season with salt and freshly ground black pepper. Place ½ cup crabmeat stuffing across the widest part of the chicken breast and fold the sides of the chicken breast around the stuffing to seal the ends. Use the plastic wrap to roll the chicken breast, forming a layer of meat around the stuffing. Wrap the plastic around the chicken roll and twist the ends to form a cylinder. Stuff and roll the remaining chicken. Place the chicken rolls on a sheet pan and freeze for 35–45 minutes to set shape. Turn the rolls over once in the freezer.

TO BREAD CHICKEN ROLLS

Set up 3 dishes or pie plates, 8 inches across by 2 to 3 inches deep. Fill the first dish with the flour seasoned with salt and freshly ground black pepper, fill the second dish with the eggs, lightly beaten, and fill the third dish with the bread crumbs mixed with the walnuts. Line a sheet pan with waxed paper to lay out the breaded chicken rolls.

Unwrap a chicken roll and coat evenly in flour. Dip the floured chicken roll into the beaten egg, lift out, and let excess egg drip back into the dish. Finally, place the chicken roll into the bread crumb and walnut mixture, pressing

(continues)

crumbs around the chicken roll to ensure the roll is well sealed. When all the chicken rolls are breaded, place them on a sheet pan, being careful to space the rolls so they are not touching. Chill the chicken rolls for 20 minutes to set the breading.

Preheat oven to 350 degrees Fahrenheit.

Once the chicken rolls are chilled, fill a large sauté pan with ½ inch of peanut oil. Heat the oil to 350 degrees Fahrenheit or use a deep fryer set at 350 degrees. Using tongs or a large slotted spoon, carefully place 2 chicken rolls in the hot oil, keeping 2 to 3 inches of space around each chicken roll. Cook the chicken rolls for 2 minutes on all 4 sides for a total of 8 minutes or until nicely browned. Add more oil to the pan as needed so that each batch of chicken rolls cooks in about ½ inch of oil.

Once all the chicken rolls have been pan-fried, arrange them on a sheet pan again, being careful to space the rolls so the sides are not touching. Place the chicken rolls in a preheated oven and bake for 15–20 minutes or until the juices run clear when rolls are pierced with the tip of a sharp knife.

TO SERVE

Allow the chicken rolls to rest for 5–10 minutes, then slice each roll into 4 or 5 pieces of equal width. Arrange the chicken slices on warm plates, drizzle with the Roasted Garlic Sauce, and serve with the Black-Eyed Pea and Sweet Potato Salad (page 267).

black-eyed pea and sweet potato salad

FOR THE DRESSING

1 medium roasted Vidalia onion
   (reserve half)
½ teaspoon olive oil
¼ cup Agrumato Lemon Oil (see note)
2 tablespoons lemon juice
2 tablespoons rice vinegar
½ teaspoon minced garlic
salt, freshly ground black pepper

⌒ NOTES

Agrumato Lemon Oil may be found in gourmet markets.

Chiffonade is a French term used to describe thin strips or shreds of herbs or vegetables.

 ERVES 8

Preheat oven to 375 degrees Fahrenheit.

TO ROAST THE ONION

Peel and trim 1 Vidalia onion and place on a 12-inch-square piece of aluminum foil. Drizzle the onion with the olive oil, close the foil loosely, and roast in a preheated oven for 1 hour or until tender. Allow the onion to cool to room temperature. Cut the onion in half and reserve half for the salad.

TO ROAST THE SWEET POTATOES

While the onion is roasting, roast the sweet potatoes . Wash the sweet potatoes and pierce each potato about 7–8 times with the tip of a sharp knife. Place the sweet potatoes on a foil-lined baking sheet and roast them for 35–40 minutes or until almost tender when pierced with a toothpick. Remove the sweet potatoes from the oven and allow them to cool to room temperature. Once the potatoes are cool, remove peels and cut into ⅓-inch dice.

DRESSING

Coarsely chop the other roasted onion half and place in a blender with the Agrumato Lemon Oil, lemon juice, vinegar, and garlic. Puree the mixture for 30–40 seconds or until smooth. Season with salt and freshly ground black pepper. Blend again for 10 seconds and then pour the dressing into small bowl and set aside.

(continues)

SALAD

In a medium-size saucepan bring 1 cup of salted water to a boil. Add the black-eyed peas and cook for 10–12 minutes or until tender. Drain the black-eyed peas in a colander, then rinse them with cold water. Allow the cooked black-eyed peas to cool to room temperature.

Roast the pepper over an open flame or under a broiler until the skin is charred. Place the roasted pepper in a paper bag and allow to steam for 10 minutes. Peel the pepper and dice.

In a large bowl combine the black-eyed peas, sweet potato, roasted pepper, and diced ham. Add the chives, jalapeño pepper, cilantro, and scallion. Gently mix all the ingredients together and drizzle with dressing. Season with salt and freshly ground black pepper. Cover the bowl and chill salad for 1 hour to blend flavors. Gently toss salad before serving.

FOR THE SALAD

2 cups fresh shelled or a 10-ounce container frozen black-eyed peas
½ medium roasted Vidalia onion, (reserved)
2 large sweet potatoes, roasted (see page 267)
1 small yellow pepper
3 ounces finely diced Smithfield ham
½ cup finely chopped chives
2 tablespoons finely diced jalapeño pepper, seeds removed
¼ cup chiffonade of cilantro (see note)
¼ cup chiffonade of scallion

FOR HERB TUILE (SEE NOTE)

⅔ cup rice flour

1 teaspoon sugar

1 teaspoon salt

4 egg whites

¼ cup heavy cream

6 tablespoons unsalted butter, melted
and cooled

1 tablespoon chopped chives

1 tablespoon chopped cilantro

freshly ground black pepper

FOR THE SALSA

2 cups finely diced pineapple

2 cups finely diced mango

1 cup finely diced tomatillos

2 tablespoons lime juice

2 tablespoons minced serrano chili

1 tablespoon chopped cilantro

½ teaspoon minced garlic

salt

~ NOTE

Baking the tuile on a Silpat mat
makes it easier to remove the tuile
from the baking surface. Silpat mats
are nonstick, reusable, silicone baking
sheets that can be found in gourmet
cookware stores.

honey-mango-glazed chicken
with spicy vegetable "noodles" and herb tuile

*S*ERVES 8

HERB TUILE

The Herb Tuile can be baked in advance and stored in an airtight container.

Combine the rice flour, sugar, and salt in a medium-size bowl and whisk to
blend. Add the egg whites all at once and whisk the mixture until smooth. Add
the cream, then pour in the cooled butter, whisking until incorporated. Stir
the chopped herbs and black pepper into the batter and chill for 20–30 minutes.

Preheat oven to 350 degrees Fahrenheit. Place rack in middle of oven.

Line an insulated baking sheet with a Silpat mat or grease and lightly flour an
insulated baking sheet. Place 1 level tablespoon of batter on one-quarter of baking sheet. Spread the batter very thinly with a small offset spatula until it is
about 4–5 inches wide and 6–7 inches long. Spread out batter for 4 tuile or less
on each baking sheet to avoid having them touch. Bake the tuile for 5 minutes,
then turn the baking sheet from front to back and continue baking for 3–4
minutes or until tuile are golden brown. Using an offset spatula, remove the
tuile from the Silpat mat to a cooling rack. Wipe Silpat with a damp paper
towel. Let the Silpat dry and the baking sheet cool before continuing to prepare
tuile. Repeat this process until all the batter is used. Handle very carefully to
avoid breaking the tuile.

PINEAPPLE TOMATILLO SALSA

*Y*IELD: APPROXIMATELY 4½ CUPS

The Pineapple Tomatillo Salsa can be prepared 2 hours ahead of serving.

Place ¼ cup each of pineapple, mango, and tomatillo in the jar of a blender.

(continues)

This piquant dish combines Asian and New World flavors. Tender chicken breasts are paired with "noodles" made of long strips of marinated vegetables and garnished with a sweet/hot fruit salsa. The herb crisp adds texture to the plate. The plate in the photograph is from the Reagan state china service.

FOR THE "NOODLES"
(SEE NOTE)

1 small sweet potato

1 small daikon radish

2 medium carrots

1 medium zucchini

1 medium yellow squash

1 small English cucumber

1 small red bell pepper

FOR THE DRESSING

½ cup rice wine vinegar

¼ cup toasted or Asian sesame oil

*2 tablespoons freshly squeezed
    lime juice*

*1 tablespoon julienne of pickled ginger
    (see note)*

1 tablespoon juice from pickled ginger

1 tablespoon chili paste

1 tablespoon chopped cilantro

2 teaspoons sugar

1 teaspoon minced garlic

salt and freshly ground black pepper

⌐ NOTES

These "noodles" are created with a Japanese chef's tool called a "Benriner Cooks Help." The Benriner cuts vegetables into long, thin spirals. If this tool is not available, use a vegetable peeler to cut long ribbons from the vegetables.

Julienne is a term used to describe cutting foods into matchstick-size strips, about 2 x ⅛ x ⅛ inches. Pickled ginger is available in Asian markets or the Asian foods section of a well-stocked supermarket.

Add the lime juice and puree until smooth. Combine the remaining pineapple, mango, and tomatillo in a large bowl. Add the serrano chili, cilantro, and garlic. Pour in the pineapple puree and mix gently. Season the salsa with salt to taste. Cover the salsa with plastic wrap and chill until ready to serve.

VEGETABLE "NOODLES"

Yield: 9–10 cups

Wash and drain and trim the ends of vegetables. Peel the sweet potato, daikon radish, and carrots. Cut all the vegetables except the red pepper into 3-inch lengths. In the Benriner use the fine cutting blade. Position a single 3-inch length of vegetable in the Benriner according to manufacturer's directions. Turn the handle and the vegetable will be cut into thin spiral strips, or "noodles." As the vegetables are cut place them into a large bowl of cold water. This helps the vegetables to curl. Continue cutting the 3-inch lengths until all the vegetables are cut into "noodles."

Remove the stem and seeds from the red pepper and cut into very thin strips. Set aside in a small bowl.

DRESSING

The dressing can be prepared 1–2 hours ahead of time.

In a 2-cup glass measure or medium-size stainless-steel bowl combine the rice wine vinegar, sesame oil, and lime juice. Add the pickled ginger and juice and the chili paste and stir to combine. Add the cilantro, sugar, and garlic and season with salt and freshly ground black pepper. Whisk all the ingredients together and set aside the dressing for the flavors to blend.

About 30 minutes before serving the Spicy Vegetable "Noodles," lift the "noodles" out of the cold water and place them in a large colander to drain.

(continues)

Toss the "noodles" every 10 minutes to drain excess water. Just prior to serving, toss the "noodles" with the dressing in a large bowl.

FOR HONEY-MANGO GLAZE

*Y*IELD: APPROXIMATELY 1½–2 CUPS

In a large, heavy-bottomed, stainless-steel or nonreactive saucepan combine the mango, honey, and chili paste. Bring the mango mixture to a simmer over low heat, stirring frequently, and cook for 15–20 minutes or until mango becomes a golden color. Add the rice wine vinegar, orange juice, and tamari and stir the mixture. Add the tomato paste, shallots, ginger, garlic, and grated orange rind. Stir until all ingredients are combined and cook over low heat for 30 minutes or until the mixture becomes the consistency of heavy syrup. While the glaze is hot ladle it through a fine-mesh strainer into a large bowl. Allow the glaze to cool to room temperature. Divide glaze in half; use half to brush chicken breasts, and use the remaining glaze to drizzle around plates just before serving.

TO PREPARE CHICKEN

Rub chicken breasts with olive oil and season with salt and freshly ground black pepper. Prepare the grill according to manufacturer's specifications. Sear the chicken breasts directly over hot coals for 2 minutes on each side. Brush each chicken breast with about 1½–2 tablespoons of glaze, making sure to brush glaze on each side. Move the chicken to a cooler part of grill and finish cooking for 6–8 minutes or until juices run clear when the chicken is pierced with the tip of a sharp knife. Remove the grilled chicken and keep warm.

FOR THE GLAZE

3 ripe mangoes, peeled and coarsely
   chopped
½ cup honey
1 tablespoon hot chili paste (see note)
1 cup rice wine vinegar
1 cup orange juice
¼ cup tamari (see note)
¼ cup tomato paste
¼ cup minced shallots
¼ cup minced ginger
1 tablespoon minced garlic
2 tablespoons grated orange rind
8 (5-ounce) boneless, skinless chicken
   breast halves
1 tablespoon olive oil
salt, freshly ground black pepper

⌒ NOTES

Hot chili paste can be purchased in Asian markets or the Asian section of some supermarkets.

Tamari is similar to soy sauce but is thicker with a mellow flavor.

TO ASSEMBLE

Toss the "noodles" with dressing and divide equally among 8 plates. Shape each pile of "noodles" into a nest and place a glazed chicken breast to one side. Garnish each plate with ½ cup Pineapple Tomatillo Salsa around the chicken and "noodles." Drizzle each plate with 2 tablespoons reserved Honey-Mango Glaze and garnish with 1 Herb Tuile. Serve remaining tuiles along with the finished plates. For a more formal presentation, cut each chicken breast into 3 or 4 slices and arrange to the side of the vegetable "noodles."

The Creole influence of Louisiana cooking can be seen in this tempting recipe. The china in the photograph is from the Franklin Delano Roosevelt state service.

2 quartered, peeled, and cored Granny
    Smith apples

1 Vidalia onion, peeled and cut into 8
    wedges

6 large, unpeeled cloves of garlic

1 tablespoon olive oil

1 tablespoon lemon juice

4 scallions, green part only

1 bunch chives

½ cup parsley leaves

1 tablespoon minced jalapeño pepper
    with seeds

⅓–½ cup chicken stock

1 teaspoon tarragon vinegar

salt, freshly ground black pepper

grilled shrimp and smoked chicken
with creole couscous and
tart apple and scallion coulis

ERVES 8

TART APPLE AND SCALLION COULIS

The Tart Apple and Scallion Coulis can be prepared 1 day in advance and stored in the refrigerator in an airtight container.

Preheat oven to 350 degrees Fahrenheit.

Combine the apples, onions, and garlic in a 9-inch square glass baking dish. Add the olive oil and lemon juice to the mixture and toss to coat. Roast the mixture, stirring 2 or 3 times, for 50–60 minutes or until apple and onion are golden brown. Remove the pan from the oven and allow to cool to room temperature. Peel the garlic and remove the hard stem ends. Place garlic, apples, and onions in the work bowl of a food processor fitted with a metal blade and puree until smooth. Scrape the puree into a medium-size bowl and set aside.

Bring a large saucepan of salted water to a boil over high heat. Blanch the scallions in boiling water for 2–3 minutes or until tender, then plunge them into a large bowl of ice water. Repeat the process, blanching the chives and parsley for 30 seconds each. Remove scallions and herbs from the ice water, squeeze out excess water, and chop coarsely.

Place the mixture in a blender and add the minced jalapeño pepper with seeds and ¼ cup of the chicken stock, vinegar, and salt and pepper. Puree the mixture, adding additional chicken stock as needed, until the mixture is smooth. Combine the scallion-herb puree with the apple-onion puree and mix well. Cover the sauce with plastic wrap and chill for 1–2 hours.

(continues)

grilled shrimp and smoked chicken, *continued*

GRILLED SHRIMP MARINADE

The shrimp in the marinade can be prepared up to 4 hours ahead of cooking time.

In a large bowl combine the oil, lemon juice, garlic, herbs, and seasonings. Mix the marinade ingredients well, add the shrimp, and toss to coat. Cover the shrimp with plastic wrap and refrigerate until ready to grill.

Prepare the shrimp for the grill by placing them on metal or water-soaked bamboo skewers. This makes cooking and turning shrimp easier. Grill the shrimp for 2 minutes on each side, on a smoking hot grill, so the shrimp cook quickly and brown nicely.

CREOLE GARNISH

Combine the vegetables and ham in a medium-size bowl and mix well. Reserve ½ cup of the Creole Garnish for final presentation. The remaining Creole Garnish is combined with some Creole Dressing and added to the couscous.

CREOLE DRESSING

In a small bowl mix together the tomato sauce, vinegar, and olive oil. Add the chopped herbs, garlic, salt, and freshly ground black pepper and mix to combine. Reserve ½ cup Creole Dressing for final presentation. Add the remaining Creole Dressing to the Creole Garnish and toss to coat. Reserve the mixture for the couscous.

CREOLE COUSCOUS

In a large saucepan with a fitted lid bring the chicken stock to a boil. Gradually add the couscous while stirring the broth. Turn off the heat and cover the saucepan. Allow the couscous to sit for 5 minutes, then add the Creole Garnish–Creole Dressing mixture and toss to combine. Cover the couscous and keep warm.

FOR THE MARINADE

2 tablespoons olive oil
2 tablespoons lemon juice
1 teaspoon minced garlic
1 tablespoon chopped basil
½ tablespoon chopped oregano
1 teaspoon crushed red pepper
salt, freshly ground black pepper
1½ pounds peeled and deveined shrimp

FOR THE GARNISH

2 ripe tomatoes, seeded and diced
1 cup finely diced celery
½ cup finely diced onion
¼ cup finely diced carrot
¼ cup finely diced red bell pepper
¼ cup finely diced yellow bell pepper
¼ cup finely diced green bell pepper
¾ cup finely diced tasso ham

FOR THE DRESSING

½ cup tomato sauce
½ cup sherry vinegar
½ cup olive oil
2 tablespoons chopped basil leaves
1 tablespoon chopped thyme leaves
1½ teaspoons minced garlic
salt, freshly ground black pepper

FOR THE COUSCOUS

3½ cups chicken stock
12 ounces couscous
2 cups Creole Garnish–Creole Dressing
    mixture

1 recipe Creole Couscous

1 pound smoked chicken breast, skinned
   and thinly sliced (see note)

½ cup Creole Dressing

1 recipe Tart Apple and Scallion Coulis

½ cup Creole Garnish

1 cup julienne of tart apple

1 cup julienne of scallion

1 recipe grilled shrimp

NOTES

Smoked chicken breast is available at gourmet markets.

Julienne is a term used to describe cutting foods into matchstick-size strips, about 2 x ⅛ x ⅛ inches.

TO ASSEMBLE

To assemble the plates, have all ingredients at hand. Warm the plates. Half fill eight 8-ounce soufflé cups with the Creole Couscous and pack lightly. Evenly divide the smoked chicken among the soufflé cups. Fill the soufflé cups to the top, packing lightly, with the remaining couscous. Place a plate over the top of a soufflé cup and turn the plate over, leaving the cup in place. Repeat with the remaining soufflé cups. Drizzle the Creole Dressing and the Tart Apple and Scallion Coulis around the plate. Sprinkle equal amounts of the Creole Garnish and the apple and scallion julienne on each plate. Carefully lift each soufflé cup away from the couscous. Top the couscous with 3 grilled shrimp per plate and serve immediately.

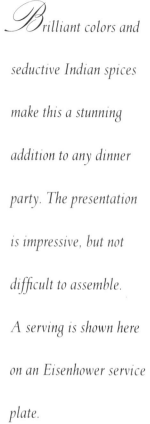

Brilliant colors and seductive Indian spices make this a stunning addition to any dinner party. The presentation is impressive, but not difficult to assemble. A serving is shown here on an Eisenhower service plate.

1½ gallons water

3 cups white wine

4 cups thinly sliced sweet onion

1 cup thinly sliced celery

1 tablespoon salt

¼ teaspoon saffron threads

1 vanilla bean, split in half

1 (3-inch) cinnamon stick

6 sprigs parsley

4 sprigs fresh thyme

1 bay leaf

15 black peppercorns, cracked

4 (1½-pound) live lobsters

poached lobster
with marinated orange salad, saffron-scented basmati rice, and emerald cilantro chutney

*S*ERVES 8

LOBSTER

The lobsters can be prepared 1 day in advance.

In a large stock or lobster pot combine the water and wine, then add the onion, celery, salt, and saffron. In cheesecloth or a spice bag, place the vanilla bean, cinnamon stick, herbs, and peppercorns. Tie off the parcel or spice bag and add it to the pot. Bring the poaching liquid to a boil over high heat. Reduce heat to medium and simmer the poaching liquid for 20–25 minutes. The liquid should be rather salty and nicely flavored by the vegetables and spices.

Ladle the poaching liquid through a strainer, discarding vegetables and spice bag, return liquid to the pot, and bring to a boil. Add the lobsters, return to a boil, and cook for 1 minute. Remove the pot from heat and let the lobsters stand in the poaching liquid until the lobsters and poaching liquid cool to room temperature; this will allow them to gently finish cooking. Storing the lobsters in the poaching liquid will keep the meat moist and infuse it with flavor.

If you do not have a pot large enough to cook all 4 lobsters at once, cook them in 2 batches. Cook the first batch for 12 minutes, then remove the lobsters from poaching liquid and set aside. Cook the second batch of lobsters for 2 minutes and allow them to cool in the poaching liquid for about 45 minutes. Add the first batch of lobsters to the cooled lobsters and poaching liquid.

Store all the lobsters in the poaching liquid in the refrigerator until ready to assemble with the Marinated Orange Salad and Saffron-Scented Basmati Rice.

(continues)

MARINATED ORANGE SALAD

The Marinated Orange Salad can be prepared 4–6 hours ahead of serving.

In a medium-size bowl combine the orange segments, radish, and cucumber. In a small bowl combine the oils, orange water, lemon juice, cumin, and cinnamon and whisk to combine. Add the dressing to the orange salad and mix gently. Add the cilantro and season with salt and freshly ground black pepper and mix gently. Cover the orange salad with plastic wrap and allow it to marinate in the refrigerator until ready to serve.

EMERALD CILANTRO CHUTNEY

*Y*IELD: I CUP; PORTION: 2 TABLESPOONS

The Emerald Cilantro Chutney can be prepared 2–3 hours ahead of time.

Combine all ingredients in the jar of a blender and puree for 10–15 seconds or until smooth. Refrigerate the Emerald Cilantro Chutney in an airtight container.

ORANGE-SAFFRON GLAZE

*Y*IELD: ½ CUP; PORTION: I TABLESPOON

The Orange-Saffron Glaze can be prepared 1–2 hours ahead of time, but do not refrigerate or the reduction will become too thick.

In a small, heavy-bottomed stainless-steel or nonreactive pot combine the orange juice and saffron. Bring the juice to a boil over medium-high heat, then reduce heat to low and simmer for 20–25 minutes or until juice is reduced to ½ cup. Allow the Orange-Saffron Glaze to cool to room temperature.

FOR THE SALAD

1 cup blood orange segments, about 6 oranges
½ cup julienne of red radishes, about 4 large radishes (see note)
1 cup julienne of English cucumber
1 tablespoon Agrumato Lemon Oil (see note)
1 tablespoon olive oil
2 teaspoons orange water
1 teaspoon lemon juice
⅛ teaspoon ground cumin
1/16 teaspoon ground cinnamon
1 tablespoon chopped cilantro leaves
salt, freshly ground black pepper

FOR THE CHUTNEY

¾ cup plain low-fat yogurt
3 tablespoons chopped cilantro
1 teaspoon chopped ginger
¼ teaspoon minced garlic
½ teaspoon ground garam masala (see note)
1/16 teaspoon ground cayenne pepper
salt

FOR THE GLAZE

2 cups freshly squeezed orange juice
¼ teaspoon saffron threads, crumbled

FOR THE SALAD

2 cups basmati rice

1 tablespoon olive oil

½ cup minced onion

¼ cup minced shallots

1 teaspoon minced garlic

1 teaspoon minced ginger

2 cups chicken stock or water

1 teaspoon rose water (see note)

¼ teaspoon saffron threads, crumbled

2 cardamom pods

3-inch stick of cinnamon

salt, white pepper

FOR THE GARNISH

⅓ cup toasted pine nuts

⅓ cup thinly sliced scallion

⅓ cup currants

3 tablespoons diced dried apricot

3 tablespoons diced dried papaya

1 teaspoon minced orange zest

½ teaspoon minced lemon zest

~ **NOTES**

Julienne is a term used to describe cutting foods into matchstick-size strips, about 2 x ⅛ x ⅛ inches.

Agrumato Lemon Oil may be found in gourmet markets.

Garam masala is a blend of dry-roasted and ground spices that can be purchased in Indian markets or in some supermarkets.

Rose water is available at gourmet and Middle Eastern markets.

SAFFRON-SCENTED BASMATI RICE SALAD

*Y*IELD: 9 CUPS

The rice can be prepared 1–2 hours in advance.

Place the rice in a medium-size bowl and cover with 4–5 cups of water. Allow the rice to soak for 30 minutes. Drain the rice in a fine-mesh strainer and wash under cool running water until the water runs clear. Drain the rice for 5–10 minutes.

Preheat oven to 350 degrees Fahrenheit.

In a large pot with a fitted lid, heat the olive oil over medium heat for 1–2 minutes. Add the onions and cook for 5–6 minutes or until translucent. Add shallots, garlic, and ginger to the onions and cook for an additional 2–3 minutes. Add the drained rice and mix well to coat rice with oil. Cook the rice for 2–3 minutes, stirring frequently so rice doesn't stick to bottom of pot. Add the stock, rose water, saffron, cardamom, and cinnamon stick. Raise heat to high and bring the rice to a boil, stirring once or twice. Cover with a lid and place the pot in the oven to bake for 18 minutes or until rice has absorbed all the liquid. Once rice is cooked, remove the cardamom pods and cinnamon stick, fluff the rice with a fork, and season with salt and white pepper. Place cooked rice in a large bowl, cool to room temperature, add the garnish ingredients, and mix well. Set the rice aside until ready to assemble plates.

TO ASSEMBLE

Have all ingredients at hand. Chill 8 large plates. Remove the lobster from the poaching liquid and discard liquid. Remove the claws and tail from each lobster, using kitchen shears. Remove the claw meat and set aside. Remove the tail in one piece by cutting shell in half lengthwise and peeling shell away from the tail. Cut tail in half lengthwise and remove the intestinal vein. Place each ½ lobster tail with one claw on a sheet pan lined with plastic wrap. Arrange 8 groups of lobster meat, 1 for each plate.

(continues)

Fill an 8-ounce soufflé cup with Saffron-Scented Basmati Rice, packing the rice lightly into the mold. Place a plate over top of the soufflé cup and turn plate over, leaving cup in place. Move the mold to center of plate and carefully remove the cup. Repeat with the remaining soufflé cups. Carefully spoon ¼ cup Marinated Orange Salad around the rice. Cut each lobster tail into 4–5 slices and carefully place lobster on top of rice salad. Top with claw meat. Drizzle 2 tablespoons of the Emerald Cilantro Chutney and 1 tablespoon of Orange-Saffron Glaze around each plate and serve immediately.

DESSERTS

Flora Bunda

Strawberries and Lemon Cream
in Chocolate Baskets

Autumn Bounty:
Rum Ice Cream in Cinnamon Phyllo Tart Shells
with Poached Pears in Red Wine
and Raspberry Sauce

Mocha Cake

Cherry Yule Log

Eggnog

FOR THE SORBET

3 cups water

2 cups sugar

1 cup fresh lemon juice, strained

FOR THE BOUQUET

1 cantaloupe

½ honeydew melon

4 kiwi fruits

2 mangoes

3 oranges

1 pint blueberries

2 pints strawberries

½ pint raspberries

1 recipe Raspberry Sauce

⌣ NOTE

The idea of this dessert is to create a "vase" out of molded lemon sorbet and a "bouquet" from fresh-cut fruit. To create the vase, use a 64-ounce plastic juice bottle as a mold for the sorbet. Cut the bottle in half lengthwise, sealing the end of the container so sorbet does not leak out.

Light but satisfying, this dessert is an impressive end to any meal. Serve it with a selection of your favorite cookies. The shape of the "vase" will depend on the shape of your freezing container. You can achieve the marble effect of the sorbet in the photograph by painting a wash of diluted liquid food coloring over the unmolded sorbet. The beaded silver tray is from the White House collection.

Serves 8

LEMON SORBET

In a large nonreactive bowl, combine the water, sugar, and lemon juice. Let the mixture stand for at least an hour, until the sugar dissolves. Once the sugar is completely dissolved, pour it into an airtight container and chill overnight in the refrigerator.

Freeze the sorbet in an ice-cream machine according to the manufacturer's directions. While the sorbet is freezing prepare the vase mold. Fill the mold with sorbet and cover with plastic wrap directly on the surface of the sorbet. Freeze sorbet mold overnight.

TO CREATE A BOUQUET OF FLOWERS USING FRESH-CUT FRUIT

CANTALOUPE

Cut a cantaloupe in half, remove the seeds, and use a melon baller to make rounds. Use the melon rounds here and there as buds.

HONEYDEW

Peel a honeydew and cut very thin wedges. Roll a thin wedge of honeydew from end to end to make a rosebud.

(continues)

KIWI

Peel and cut a kiwi in half through the center, as a lemon is cut to form two crowns. Cut the kiwi crowns in half lengthwise so they lie flat to form a tulip.

MANGO

Peel a mango, remove the pit, and cut into very thin slices. Roll a few slices to form a bud. Roll several more mango slices to form a flower.

ORANGES

Cut away the rind from an orange and cut the orange into segments. Arrange the orange segments like flower petals, then place several blueberries in center to form a black-eyed Susan.

STRAWBERRIES

Remove stems from strawberries and make several partial cuts to create a fan.

Fruit can be cut, shaped, and laid out on a tray lined with plastic wrap. Cover the prepared fruit with a damp towel and refrigerate until ready to create a bouquet.

Have the fruit ready to arrange quickly as the sorbet is unmolded. Unmold the sorbet onto a well-chilled oval platter. Arrange the fruit bouquet on the platter so it is coming from the top of vase. Once the bouquet is arranged, sprinkle with additional blueberries and raspberries for color accents and serve immediately. The Flora Bunda may be served with the Raspberry Sauce on the side.

RASPBERRY SAUCE

*Y*IELD: 1¼ CUPS (APPROXIMATELY)

In the work bowl of a food processor fitted with a metal blade, add the raspberries and preserves and pulse until smooth. Working over a medium-size bowl, pour the sauce through a fine-mesh strainer. Use a rubber spatula to push the sauce through, wipe the seeds from the spatula, and then scrape off the bottom of the strainer. Add the framboise, mix to combine, cover with plastic wrap, and chill until serving time.

FOR THE SAUCE

12 ounces fresh raspberries or a 12-ounce package frozen unsweetened raspberries
½ cup raspberry preserves
2 tablespoons framboise or raspberry eau-de-vie, optional

5 *pints whole strawberries (see note)*

1 *cup water*

1 *cup plus 2 tablespoons sugar*

3 *tablespoons light corn syrup*

NOTES

The strawberry syrup is a nice sweetener for iced tea or lemonade. The syrup can also be used to brush on cake layers before frosting.

When preparing the chocolate baskets, have a few microwave-safe glass measures or bowls and clean, dry pastry brushes on hand. Alternately, wash and dry the glass measure and pastry brush after each coat of chocolate.

strawberries and lemon cream
in chocolate baskets

A version of this dessert, a delectable mixture of ripe strawberries, lemon curd, and whipped cream, was served at the State Dinner in honor of United Kingdom Prime Minister Tony Blair. Pastry Chef Mesnier created a large chocolate basket decorated with molded chocolate reliefs and spun-sugar flowers; the recipe here gives the home cook instructions for making individual baskets. You could also serve this in your prettiest glass bowl, accompanied by shortbread cookies. The basket is shown on a plate from the Truman state china service.

YIELD: 8 BASKETS

This dessert can be prepared 1 day ahead and assembled at serving time. The strawberries in syrup should be prepared a minimum of 6 hours ahead but preferably 1 day ahead of serving time so the berries will have a chance to macerate in the sugar.

STRAWBERRIES IN SYRUP

Wash the strawberries and spread them out on paper towels to dry. Hull the strawberries and place them in a medium-size bowl, leaving them at room temperature while preparing the syrup.

In a small, heavy-bottomed saucepan combine the water, sugar, and corn syrup. Bring the mixture to a boil over medium heat, stirring to dissolve the sugar. Once the sugar has dissolved, clamp a candy thermometer to the inside of the saucepan. Reduce the heat, if necessary, to prevent the syrup from boiling over. Boil the syrup for 25–35 minutes or until it reaches 250–260 degrees Fahrenheit on a candy thermometer. Pour the hot syrup over the

(continues)

strawberries and allow the mixture to cool to room temperature. The sugar will get crusty and then melt and dissolve as it cools. Cover the strawberries with plastic wrap and refrigerate overnight.

FOR THE LEMON CURD

The lemon curd can be prepared 1–2 days in advance and stored in the refrigerator in an airtight container with plastic wrap covering the surface of the curd.

In a medium-size, heavy-bottomed, nonreactive pot combine the lemon juice, grated rind, and sugar. Mix well. Add the eggs and whisk the mixture to blend. Add the butter all at once and stir. Place the pot over medium heat and, whisking gently, slowly bring the mixture to a boil. Continue whisking to prevent the eggs from scrambling. It should take 4–5 minutes for the mixture to come to a boil and thicken.

Strain the lemon curd through a fine-mesh strainer into a glass bowl and cover with plastic wrap directly on surface to prevent a skin from forming.

CHOCOLATE BASKETS

The baskets can be prepared 1–2 days in advance and stored in an airtight plastic container until ready to assemble desserts.

Place ⅔ cup chopped chocolate in a microwave-safe glass measure or bowl. Microwave the chocolate on 50 percent power for 30 seconds, then allow it to sit for 10 seconds and microwave for 2 more 30-second intervals with a 10-second rest. The chocolate should be two-thirds of the way melted. Stir gently until smooth, being careful not to incorporate air bubbles in the chocolate. Check the temperature with an instant-read thermometer; the chocolate should be about 88–90 degrees Fahrenheit. To keep the chocolate at this temperature, place the glass measure or bowl in a shallow bowl of warm water. Work carefully because the chocolate will seize if spattered with water.

FOR THE LEMON CURD

½ cup fresh lemon juice
2 tablespoons finely grated lemon rind
1¼ cups sugar
3 large eggs
10 tablespoons unsalted butter, room temperature, cut into 1-inch pieces

FOR THE CHOCOLATE BASKETS

½ pound finely chopped semisweet chocolate (approximately 2 cups)
8 large muffin papers, 3½–4 inches diameter

1–2 pints whole strawberries, washed and hulled
1½ cups heavy cream

Set the muffin papers into muffin tins or 1-cup custard cups. Using a clean, dry pastry brush, coat the sides of the muffin papers, working from the bottom to the top, but do not brush chocolate over the edge of the muffin paper. Coat the bottoms last. Brush all the muffin papers using all the tempered chocolate. Chill chocolate "baskets" while preparing another ⅔ cup or another recipe of chopped chocolate in a clean, dry glass measure or bowl. Repeat brushing the baskets with chocolate 2 more times for a total of 3 chocolate layers. Chill the baskets after the final layer of chocolate for a minimum of 2 hours.

TO ASSEMBLE

Drain the strawberries and allow them to sit in the strainer for 15–20 minutes. Reserve strawberry syrup for another use. Chill the heavy cream in a mixing bowl and chill the whisk or beaters as well. Remove the muffin papers from outside of the chocolate baskets, and place each basket on a chilled dessert plate. Whip the chilled cream on medium speed until soft peaks form. Place 1½ cups lemon curd in a medium-size bowl and stir to soften, fold the whipped cream into the curd, taste, and add more lemon curd if desired. Fold in the drained strawberries. Spoon the lemon cream in equal amounts into each chocolate basket. Garnish with fresh strawberries and serve immediately.

A spun-sugar flower adorns the basket of strawberries. If you're not a candy maker, you can put a silk flower on an edible dessert—or how about an edible flower?

FOR THE PEARS

3 cups red wine

2¼ cups sugar

1 (12-ounce) package frozen,
    unsweetened raspberries

1 cup water

4 (3-inch) cinnamon sticks

2 teaspoons whole black peppercorns

8 whole cloves

1 strip lemon peel, about 3 × 1 inches

1 strip orange peel, about 3 × 1 inches

8 small, ripe pears (see note)

2 lemons, cut in half

2 tablespoons cornstarch

2 tablespoons water

NOTES

A California Merlot is an excellent choice for poaching these pears, but any red wine with fruit notes would also be a good choice.

These pears are served whole, so select nicely shaped D'Anjou, Bartlett, or Bosc pears with stems.

Poach the pears in a heavy-bottomed, nonreactive pot that can hold them all in a single layer while cooking.

autumn bounty
rum ice cream in cinnamon phyllo tart shells with poached pears in red wine and raspberry sauce

*S*ERVES 8

POACHED PEARS

In a medium-size, nonreactive saucepan combine the wine, sugar, raspberries, and water. Add the cinnamon sticks, peppercorns, cloves, lemon peel, and orange peel to the pot. Bring the mixture to a boil over medium heat, stirring to dissolve the sugar. Reduce the heat to medium low and simmer for 15–20 minutes or until the raspberries are soft and spices have infused the wine.

Peel the pears and squeeze a little lemon juice over each pear to prevent them from turning brown. Place the peeled pears in a larger pot. When the poaching syrup is cooked, strain it through a fine-mesh strainer over the pears. Press the raspberries to force some puree through the sieve. Discard the seeds and spices.

Gently stir the pears to coat with the poaching syrup. Bring the syrup to a boil over medium heat; this will take 15–20 minutes. Once the syrup has begun to boil, reduce the heat to low and simmer the pears for 3–5 minutes. Turn off the heat and allow the pears to finish cooking in the poaching syrup as it cools to room temperature. For larger pears or pears that are not quite ripe, cook about 12–15 minutes or until tender when pierced with the tip of a sharp knife.

Store the pears in the poaching syrup in an airtight container for up to 2 days. Carefully remove the pears from the syrup 2–3 hours before serving, place on a large plate, cover with plastic wrap and refrigerate. Pour the sauce into a medium-size, nonreactive saucepan and, over medium heat, bring to a boil.

(continues)

t the White House,

a mold of rum ice cream

is crowned with a golden

pastry shell and

surrounded by wine-

poached pears and fresh

raspberries, shown here on

the Wilson state china.

The instructions in the

recipe are for individual

servings: a pastry cup

filled with ice cream and

accompanied by a pear for

each diner.

FOR THE ICE CREAM

2 cups whole milk

8 large egg yolks

½ cup plus 1 tablespoon sugar

1 cup golden raisins

¼ cup plus 2 tablespoons dark rum

¼ cup heavy cream

Place the cornstarch in a small bowl, add 2 tablespoons water, and stir until smooth. In a thin stream, pour the cornstarch into the boiling sauce, whisking constantly to prevent the sauce from sticking to the bottom of pan. Cook the sauce for 2 minutes, continuing to whisk. Once the sauce has thickened, strain it into a medium-size bowl and cool to room temperature.

RUM ICE CREAM

Pour milk into a nonreactive saucepan. Over low heat, bring it barely to a simmer. While milk is heating, combine the egg yolks and sugar in a medium-size bowl and whisk until smooth. When the milk is about to simmer, pour a small amount into the egg yolk mixture while whisking. Gradually add all the milk and whisk to blend. Return the milk and egg yolk mixture to the saucepan and cook over low heat for 4–5 minutes. Whisk the mixture constantly to prevent the egg yolks from scrambling. When the custard coats the back of a spoon and a finger drawn across leaves a path, immediately remove from heat. Strain the custard into a bowl and cover with plastic wrap directly on surface of custard to prevent a skin from forming. Chill for a minimum of 3–4 hours or overnight.

Combine the golden raisins and 2 tablespoons rum and allow the raisins to plump for 1 hour. In a small sauté pan warm raisins and rum over low heat. Ignite the rum with a long kitchen or fireplace match, shake pan very gently, and allow the rum to burn off. Remove the raisins from the heat, pour into a small bowl, and chill for about 1 hour.

Once raisins are chilled, add heavy cream and ¼ cup rum to the chilled milk and egg mixture. Freeze the mixture in an ice-cream machine according to the manufacturer's directions. When the ice cream is frozen, fold in the raisins and pack the ice cream into a 2-quart container. Freeze the ice cream for 6–8 hours or overnight.

(continues)

CINNAMON PHYLLO TART SHELLS

Cover the phyllo dough with plastic wrap and a damp towel to prevent dough from drying out. Combine the sugar and cinnamon in a small bowl and mix well. Lightly grease 8 custard cups or a 12-cup muffin tin.

Lay out a sheet of phyllo, brush it with melted butter, and sprinkle on 1 tablespoon cinnamon sugar, repeating this with all layers. Brush the top layer with butter, but do not sprinkle with cinnamon sugar.

Trim the phyllo layers to a 16 x 8-inch rectangle. Cut the phyllo in half lengthwise to form two 16 x 4-inch strips. Cut each strip into four 4-inch-square pieces. Press the phyllo squares into the greased cups of a muffin tin, leaving the corners sticking up above the rim for a whimsical shape. Freeze the tart shells for 10–15 minutes.

Preheat oven to 325 degrees Fahrenheit.

Bake the tart shells for 8–10 minutes or until golden brown. Allow the tart shells to cool in the pan for 5 minutes. Carefully remove the shells to a cooling rack to cool completely.

TO SERVE

Carefully remove the pear cores by scooping out bottom of each pear with a melon baller. Trim bottom of each pear so it sits straight on a plate. Arrange each pear on a chilled dessert plate alongside a Cinnamon Phyllo Tart Shell filled with Rum Ice Cream. Drizzle the plates with equal amounts of the Red Wine and Raspberry Sauce and serve immediately.

FOR THE TART SHELLS

4 sheets phyllo dough, 12 × 18 inches each
⅓ cup sugar
½ teaspoon ground cinnamon
8 tablespoons melted butter

mocha cake

FOR THE CAKE

4 large eggs, room temperature

½ cup plus 1 tablespoon sugar

1 tablespoon instant espresso powder

1 tablespoon hot water

1 cup flour, sifted

4 tablespoons butter, melted and cooled
   to room temperature

FOR THE BUTTERCREAM

2 cups whole milk

1¼ cups ground coffee

1⅓ cups sugar

6 large egg yolks

1 pound unsalted butter, softened

1 cup walnuts, toasted and chopped

NOTE

Use the coffee of your choice to
flavor the buttercream and the syrup.

SERVES 12

CAKE

Preheat oven to 350 degrees Fahrenheit. Butter and flour a 9 x 3-inch round cake pan. Combine the eggs and sugar in the bowl of a stand mixer. Place the bowl over a large pot of simmering water, making sure the bottom of the bowl is not in contact with the water. Gently whisk the mixture by hand until the eggs reach a temperature of 98–99 degrees Fahrenheit.

Transfer the bowl to a stand mixer and whip the egg mixture on high for 7 minutes. Reduce speed to medium and continue whipping the eggs for 5 minutes or until fluffy and lemon-colored.

While the eggs are beating, dissolve the espresso powder in hot water. When the eggs have tripled in volume, gently fold in the dissolved espresso. Add half the sifted flour and fold it gently into the eggs. Repeat with the remaining flour and fold in the melted butter.

Pour the batter into the prepared cake pan and smooth the top with a small spatula.

Bake for 23–25 minutes or until the cake begins to pull away from the sides of the pan and it springs back when touched gently in the center. Cool in the pan for 5 minutes, turn the cake out, and cool completely on a wire rack.

MOCHA BUTTERCREAM

Combine the milk and ground coffee in a medium-size saucepan. While stirring, bring the mixture to a boil over low heat. Strain the milk into a 2-cup glass measure. Add more milk if necessary, to equal 1½ cups.

Pour the coffee milk into a clean saucepan, add ⅔ cup sugar, and bring to a simmer over medium heat, stirring occasionally.

(continues)

Decadently rich, this buttercream-filled and -frosted cake is displayed here on a magnificent piece of sugar art. The flowers are a fantasy creation of Pastry Chef Mesnier's that he calls the "Hillary Rose."

FOR THE SYRUP

½ cup brewed coffee (see note)

2 tablespoons sugar

2 tablespoons Kahlúa or coffee liqueur,
*   optional*

In a large bowl combine the egg yolks and remaining ⅔ cup sugar. Whisk until the yolks are smooth. When the coffee milk comes to a simmer pour a small amount over yolks, whisking continuously. Gradually add all the milk to the yolks, whisking to mix well.

Return the milk and yolk mixture to the saucepan and cook for 5–6 minutes over medium heat, stirring constantly with a wooden spoon. When the mixture coats the back of the spoon and a finger drawn across leaves a path, immediately remove from heat. Strain the custard into a large bowl, cover with plastic wrap directly on surface of custard, and cool to room temperature.

When the custard is cooled put the softened butter into the bowl of a stand mixer. Whip butter at medium speed until very light and fluffy. In a steady stream, gradually pour the custard into the butter. When all of the custard is incorporated, scrape down the sides of bowl and mix for an additional minute.

TO ASSEMBLE

Measure height of the cake and mark 3 equal layers with toothpicks around the outside edge. Cut the cake into even layers, using the toothpicks as a guide.

In a small bowl combine the brewed coffee, sugar, and Kahlúa. Place the bottom of the cake on a 10-inch plate or 9-inch cardboard circle. Brush the layer with coffee syrup. Spread 1 cup buttercream on the layer and sprinkle with ½ cup nuts. Repeat with the middle layer. For the top layer, brush syrup on the cut side of the layer before placing it on top of the buttercream and nuts.

Spread about ½ cup buttercream in a thin layer around the outside of cake and chill for 30 minutes. This prevents crumbs from getting into the buttercream as you decorate the cake. Once the cake is chilled, spread 1 cup buttercream on top and sides and smooth the frosting. Use a pastry bag and a small star tip to decorate the cake with remaining buttercream.

Chill the cake for 2–3 hours. Remove the cake from refrigerator and allow it to sit at room temperature for 1 hour before serving.

cherry yule log

$\mathscr{S}$ERVES 8

PLAN FOR CHERRY YULE LOG

The Cherry Yule Log can be prepared in stages. Start by preparing the Chocolate Sponge Cake. The cake can be baked and cut shortly after it comes out of the oven, then covered and stored at room temperature overnight.

CHOCOLATE SPONGE CAKE

Preheat oven to 400 degrees Fahrenheit.

Grease a 15 x 10 x 1-inch jelly roll pan and line the bottom with parchment paper, greasing the parchment paper as well. Sift together the flour and cocoa powder and set aside.

Combine the egg yolks and ¼ cup plus 1 tablespoon sugar in the bowl of a stand mixer. Place the bowl over a large pot of simmering water, making sure the bottom of the bowl is not in contact with the water. Gently whisk the mixture by hand until the eggs yolks reach a temperature of 98–99 degrees Fahrenheit.

Transfer the bowl to a stand mixer and whip the egg yolk mixture on high for 7 minutes or until pale yellow and yolks form a ribbon when the whisk attachment is lifted from the bowl. Set aside the egg yolk mixture.

In a separate large bowl, using a handheld mixer, whip the egg whites on medium speed until soft peaks form. Turn the mixer to high and whip the egg whites, adding the remaining sugar 1 tablespoon at a time. Whip the egg whites until stiff peaks form and the sugar is dissolved.

Combine the dry ingredients in 2 additions and the egg whites in 3 additions. Sift half of the flour mixture over the egg yolks, folding gently. Add one-third of the egg whites and fold into the batter. Sift and fold the remaining flour into

FOR THE YULE LOG

1 recipe Chocolate Sponge Cake
1 recipe Syrup
1 recipe Cherry Mousse
1 recipe Chocolate Mousse
1 recipe Chocolate Ganache
1 recipe Crème Anglaise
2 pounds fresh bing cherries, pitted

FOR THE SPONGE CAKE

½ cup flour
¼ cup plus 1 tablespoon cocoa powder
4 large eggs, separated
½ cup plus 2 tablespoons sugar, divided

⌒ NOTES

This recipe uses a deerback mold to shape the cake into a Yule log. Originally from Austria, the deerback mold is shaped like a half-moon, measures about 12 x 4 x 2 inches, and holds about 4½ cups. It can be found in specialty baking stores.

Prepare each mousse only when the cake is ready to be filled.

Use a pastry brush and cover the cake with the Chocolate Ganache to create a "bark" texture for the Yule log.

Layers of cherry and chocolate mousse are encased in a chocolate sponge cake shell, covered with chocolate ganache, and served with a crème anglaise (custard sauce). Decorations are up to you; here Pastry Chef Mesnier has used marzipan deer, molded chocolate trees and leaves, and cherries as a garnish.

FOR THE SYRUP

½ cup sugar
¼ cup water

FOR THE CHERRY MOUSSE

⅔ cup heavy cream
1 cup pitted sour cherries
¼ cup cherry juice
⅛ teaspoon almond extract
¼ cup sugar
2 teaspoons unflavored gelatin

the batter. Add one-third more egg whites to batter and fold gently. Finish the batter by folding in the remaining egg whites. Scrape the batter into a prepared pan and smooth into an even layer using a small offset spatula. Bake the cake for 10–12 minutes or until the cake begins to pull away from the sides of the pan and it springs back when touched gently in the center. Cool in pan for 5 minutes.

Use a small sharp knife to loosen cake from sides of the pan. Turn the cake out onto a cutting board. Carefully remove the parchment paper and trim ½ inch from the edges of the cake.

FOR THE SYRUP

In a small, heavy-bottomed saucepan, combine the sugar and water and bring to a boil over medium heat. Stir to dissolve the sugar. Reduce the heat to low and simmer for 5 minutes. Remove from heat and cool to room temperature.

CHERRY MOUSSE

Whip the cream until soft peaks form, and chill in the refrigerator. Combine the cherries and 2 tablespoons cherry juice in the jar of a blender. Add the almond extract and sugar and puree for 1 minute or until smooth. Strain the mixture through a fine-mesh strainer into a medium-size bowl. Place the remaining 2 tablespoons cherry juice in a small microwave-safe glass bowl and sprinkle with the gelatin. When gelatin has dissolved, microwave it on 30 percent power for 15 seconds. Stir and, if necessary, microwave an additional 10 seconds. Whisk the melted gelatin into the cherry puree and set the bowl into a large bowl one-quarter full of ice water. Gently stir the cherry puree until it begins to thicken. Remove the bowl of puree from the ice and carefully fold in the chilled whipped cream.

FOR THE CHOCOLATE MOUSSE

1 cup heavy cream

1 cup chopped semisweet chocolate

FOR THE GANACHE

1½ cups chopped semisweet chocolate

⅓ cup heavy cream

1 tablespoon light corn syrup

FOR THE CRÈME ANGLAISE

6 large egg yolks

4 tablespoons sugar

1½ cups milk

1 vanilla bean, split

⌐ NOTE

If storing the Crème Anglaise, strain it before serving.

CHOCOLATE MOUSSE

Whip the cream in a medium-size bowl until soft peaks form. Set the cream aside at room temperature. Melt the chocolate in a microwave-safe glass bowl at 50 percent power for 30 seconds. Allow the chocolate to sit for 10 seconds. Microwave again for 30 seconds and stir until the chocolate is smooth. Gradually add the melted chocolate to the whipped cream, folding the chocolate into the cream.

CHOCOLATE GANACHE

Place the chopped chocolate in a medium-size bowl. In a small pot combine the cream and corn syrup and bring to a simmer. Pour the hot cream over the chopped chocolate and allow the mixture to sit for 30 seconds. Stir the ganache until all the chocolate has melted and the mixture is smooth.

CRÈME ANGLAISE

*Y*IELD: SCANT 2 CUPS

Crème Anglaise can be stored in the refrigerator in an airtight container for up to 2 days.

In a medium-size bowl, whisk the egg yolks and 2 tablespoons sugar until the mixture forms a ribbon when the whisk is lifted from bowl. In a heavy-bottomed saucepan bring the milk to a boil with the remaining sugar and the vanilla bean. Pour the hot milk into the egg yolk mixture while whisking. Return the milk and egg yolk mixture to the saucepan and cook over medium heat, stirring constantly with a wooden spoon. When the mixture coats the back of the spoon and a finger drawn across leaves a path, immediately remove from heat. Strain the Crème Anglaise into a bowl. Scrape the seeds from the vanilla bean into the Crème Anglaise, cover with plastic wrap, and chill.

(continues)

TO ASSEMBLE

Line the deerback mold with the Chocolate Sponge Cake by placing the mold lengthwise over two-thirds of the cake. Trim the excess cake, approximately a 3-inch strip, and reserve for another use. Cut a strip of cake the same size as the bottom of the mold, about 11 x 3 ½ inches. Use the remaining 11 x 7-inch piece of cake to line the mold.

Brush the cake in the mold with Syrup. Prepare the Cherry Mousse (see page 300). Fill the mold half-full of Cherry Mousse and pour any remaining mousse into a small dessert cup to enjoy later. Chill the cake, allowing the Cherry Mousse to set for 1 hour or until firm.

Prepare the Chocolate Mousse (see page 301). Fill the mold to the top with the Chocolate Mousse and cover the mousse with the remaining 11 x 3 ½-inch strip of chocolate sponge cake. Brush the cake with Syrup. Cover the cake with plastic wrap and refrigerate for 1 hour.

Prepare the Chocolate Ganache (see page 301). Turn the cake out of the mold onto a rack set over a sheet pan. Spread the ganache over cake in an even layer, using a pastry brush to create a barklike texture. Chill the Cherry Yule Log for 30 minutes before serving.

TO SERVE

Place the Cherry Yule Log on a serving platter and garnish with pitted bing cherries. Slice the Yule log with a serrated knife, wiping the knife clean after each slice. Pour equal amounts of Crème Anglaise onto 8 chilled dessert plates and carefully place a Yule log slice on each plate. Garnish the plates with a few bing cherries and serve immediately.

eggnog

4 large eggs, separated (see note)

1 cup sugar

½ cup plus 2 tablespoons bourbon

½ cup plus 2 tablespoons cognac

½ cup plus 2 tablespoons dark rum

½ teaspoon salt

2 cups heavy cream

1 teaspoon vanilla

½ teaspoon nutmeg

1 quart milk

NOTE

Raw eggs present a risk of salmonella exposure and should not be consumed by the very young, the very old, or anyone with a compromised immune system.

Executive Chef Walter Scheib is responsible for the White House Eggnog, as much a dessert as it is a drink. A cup of Eggnog and a slice of Cherry Yule Log will make your Christmas merry and bright.

YIELD: APPROXIMATELY 3 QUARTS

Use pasteurized whites and yolks. If this product is not available, eggs should be fresh and from a reliable source. This Eggnog is chilled before serving and can sit at room temperature, in a punch bowl, but should be discarded after 4–5 hours.

In the bowl of a stand mixer combine yolks and sugar. Whip on medium speed for 3–4 minutes or until the yolk mixture forms a ribbon when the whisk is lifted out of the bowl. At low speed gradually add the bourbon, cognac, and rum. The mixture will become thinner.

In a very large bowl combine the egg whites and salt. Using a handheld mixer, beat on medium speed until foamy. Increase the mixer speed to high and beat until soft peaks form.

In a medium-size bowl whip the cream until soft peaks form. Fold the yolk mixture into the egg whites, then fold in the whipped cream, vanilla, and nutmeg. Add the milk and mix well.

Chill the Eggnog for 2–3 hours. When ready to serve whisk the Eggnog to incorporate foam on surface.

CREDITS

METRIC EQUIVALENCIES

LIQUID AND DRY MEASURE EQUIVALENCIES

CUSTOMARY	METRIC	CUSTOMARY	METRIC
¼ teaspoon	1.25 milliliters	1 pint (2 cups)	480 milliliters
½ teaspoon	2.5 milliliters	1 quart (4 cups)	960 milliliters (.96 liter)
1 teaspoon	5 milliliters	1 gallon (4 quarts)	3. 84 liters
1 tablespoon	15 milliliters		
1 fluid ounce	30 milliliters		
¼ cup	60 milliliters	1 ounce (by weight)	28 grams
⅓ cup	80 milliliters	¼ pound (4 ounces)	114 grams
½ cup	120 milliliters	1 pound (16 ounces)	454 grams
1 cup	240 milliliters	2.2 pounds	1 kilogram (1000 grams)

OVEN-TEMPERATURE EQUIVALENCIES

DESCRIPTION	°FAHRENHEIT	°CELSIUS
Cool	200	90
Very slow	250	120
Slow	300–325	150–160
Moderately slow	325–350	160–180
Moderate	350–375	180–190
Moderately hot	375–400	190–200
Hot	400–450	200–230
Very hot	450–500	230–260

ACKNOWLEDGMENTS

I am grateful:

To those people who care for the people's house, including Gary Walters and the residence staff, and the National Park Service, led by Interior Secretary Bruce Babbitt and Director Bob Stanton;

To those who have helped us welcome the world, including Ann Stock, Capricia Marshall, Walter Scheib, Christeta Comerford, John Moeller, Roland Mesnier, Franette McCullough, Nancy Clarke, Mel French, Molly Raiser, Sharon Kennedy, Kim Widdess, Tracy LeBreque Davis, Robin Dickey, Emily Feingold, Sarah Farnsworth, Ann McCoy, Laura Schwartz, Debby McGinn, Tibbie Turner, Rick Paulus, and their talented and tireless colleagues;

To those who have preserved the house for history, including Betty Monkman, Rex Scouten, and their staffs, Neil Horstman and the White House Historical Association, the members of the Committee for the Preservation of the White House, and the supporters of the White House Endowment Fund;

To those in the Office of the First Lady and the White House Millennium Council who have helped us celebrate America, including Maggie Williams, Melanne Verveer, Shirley Sagawa, Bobbie Greene, Ellen McCulloch Lovell, Anne Donovan, Laura Schiller, MaryEllen McGuire, Neel Lattimore, Pam Cicetti, Lissa Muscatine, Eric Woodard, Kim Henry, Nicole Rabner, Patti Solis Doyle, Kelly Craighead, Jen Klein, Ann O'Leary, Marsha Berry, Huma Abedin, Alice Pushkar, and the rest of the staff and volunteers;

To those in the White House Photo Office who have recorded events behind the scenes and in the public eye, including photographers Sharon Farmer, Bob McNeely, Ralph Alswang, William Vasta, David Scull, Barbara Kinney, and Callie Shell; Marilyn Jacanin, David Hicks, Lori Wiener, Janet Philips, and the staff in the photo lab;

To the President's staff who make history happen, led by Chiefs of Staff Mack McLarty, Leon Panetta, Erskine Bowles, and John Podesta;

To those who have helped me open the doors of the people's house to the readers of this book, especially editor Sydny Miner, Carolyn Reidy, David Rosenthal, Irene Yohay, Andrea Mullins, Jackie Seow, Amy Hill, O'Lanso Gabbidon, Bonni Leon, Patty Bozza, Karen Romano, Jim Thiel, Bob Barnett, and Phillippa Polskin; photographers Robert Clark, Todd Eberle, Romulo Yanes, William Everett, David Finn, and Diana Walker, and their assistants and studio staff; designer and adviser Kaki Hockersmith; food stylists Marianne Sauvion and Grady Best; Cheryl Merser, Christine Hagstrom, Claire Turner, and Carol Beach, for their assistance with the text; and Carl Anthony and J. Carter Brown, for their warm words;

And most of all, to Bill and Chelsea, and our family and friends, who have made this house a home.

INDEXES

RECIPE INDEX

Page numbers in *italics*
refer to illustrations.